THE PR

OF

THE RELIGIOUS LIFE

OR

AN EXPLICATION OF

THE CATECHISM OF THE VOWS.

BY

THE REV. PETER COTEL, S. J.

TRANSLATED FROM THE FRENCH BY

L. W. REILLY.

Imprimatur:

J. Card. Gibbons.

Arch. Balt.

Baltimore, Feb. 26th, 1894.

TABLE OF CONTENTS.

PART II.

THE THREE VOWS OF RELIGION IN PARTICULAR.

INTRODUCTION.

It is not hard to show that all the principles of the religious life are connected with the profession of the vows that are made therein; because these vows already include its chief obligations; and any explanation of them, done as it should be, even though brief, inevitably touches all the others.

Now, in the little treatise which we published under the title, "The Catechism of the Vows," our purpose was only to state very briefly these principles and these obligations of the religious life. It was simply an elementary work which we designed for all persons who live in the religious state, and we hoped that its usefulness would be all the more general, for the reason that its very brevity would make it easy to learn and to remember. And, as it turned out, we have had the consolation to see the little book find its way, in the course of a few years, into a large number of religious communities.

But a Catechism usually makes necessary an explication. On the other hand, it cannot tell everything to the teachers of it, who, nevertheless, have need, in order to expound an abridgment with more confidence and profit, to know beyond what it contains. Accordingly, a number of persons, whose duty it is to explain to others "The Catechism of the Vows," have expressed to us their regret that questions of such importance were presented by it with such conciseness. At least they would be glad to find elsewhere the same subjects with developments apt to elucidate them.

We have tried to meet their need by the publication of this new volume. Instead of confining ourselves to the plan of indicating the distinguished writers who treat of these matters, and of letting every one have the trouble of hunting here and there for the quotations which they want, we have, as it were, placed these in their hands, in the same order in which they were referred to in the Catechism itself; and without repeating the points, which, in our judgment, are there sufficiently set forth, we have here added whatever has seemed to us to be required for an understanding of the others.

Among the authorities whom we summon to the support of our statements, the Angel of the Schools, Saint Thomas, is the one that we cite most often and most gladly, because, in religious questions, no teaching is more sure, more lucid, or more full than his. It is true that, because of this reliance on the Angelic Doctor, there results a teaching whose gravity is not equally accessible to all persons; but those for whom we intend it principally will know how to accommodate it to the intelligence of those whom they are instructing in it.

TRANSLATOR'S PREFACE.

THE number of persons in this country following the evangelical counsels has marvelously increased within the past decade by reason of the recent introduction of Congregations from abroad, and by the spread of the Orders that have long been here. And lately, too, a notable fertility of vocations has crowded novitiates with postulants prospecting the way of perfection, and eager to mount to its loftiest heights. Therefore the publication of this treatise is most opportune. For every person in religion—novice or professed, subject or superior—needs to know precisely how far the conscience is bound by the vows of that holy state, the means of spiritual progress that it offers, the obligations and the privileges of the celestial call to it, and the other principles of the religious life. This information is all here, and is set forth with luminous simplicity.

Other authors have treated this same subject, but the works of only a few of them are accessible to American readers, nor have they all the clearness, the accuracy and brevity that distinguish the production of the Rev. Father Cotel. These qualities have made his book so popular in France that it has passed through several editions and won for it unstinted praise from most competent judges.

That this English version may approach the usefulness of the original, is the heartfelt wish of

THE TRANSLATOR.

HANOVER, MD., March 25, 1894.

The Principles of the Religious Life;

OR, THE EXPLANATION OF THE

CATECHISM OF THE VOWS.

———

PART FIRST.

ON THE VOWS OF RELIGION IN GENERAL.

The object of this first part is to explain the most fundamental principles of the religious life. The little "Catechism of the Vows" could, as it were, only point out these principles; we shall now endeavor to give them all the light which their importance requires.

———

CHAPTER I.

GENERAL IDEA OF THE VOW, CONSIDERED IN THE VOWS OF RELIGION.

——

ARTICLE I.

DEFINITION OF THE VOW.

A vow is defined as *a deliberate promise made to God of an act better than its opposite.*

Let us consider the great practical lessons that spring from this definition.

1

Section I.—*The Vow is a Promise.*

Among the promises which men are wont to make among themselves, three kinds may be distinguished; the simple promise, the promise of honor, and the promise of contract. In the first, a man binds himself but with this mental reservation: "If I can do so easily, if no obstacle arise." In the second, the word given involved the man's honor; a serious impediment would be required for him to believe himself and for him to be considered by others free from this engagement. But the third promise, once legitimately made and accepted, constitutes a formal claim of justice; failure to keep it renders a person liable to be cited to court.

Very nearly the same may be said of the promises we make to the Lord. It may be a simple promise, as for example, to undertake in order to please Him some supererogatory work of piety. The same reservation is implied, namely: "If nothing hinders me," or, at least I have no intention to bind myself under pain of sin.

We often make to God the promise of fulfilling towards Him an already existing obligation. It is a *resolution* we thus formulate in His presence, for the purpose of exciting ourselves to do our duty; it is no new obligation that we intend to impose upon ourselves.

Sometimes adding solemnity to this acknowledgment of an engagement already contracted,

we protest before witnesses that our will is to
fulfill it: it then becomes like a promise of
honor, the effect of which is to tighten the
bond of conscience, but not to double it; such
are the promises of baptism, improperly called
vows; such is especially the public renewal of
them made in certain circumstances of life;
such also is the ceremony of the renovation of
vows when they have not ceased to exist. No
new obligation is imposed thereby on the con·
science.

A promise made to God that may properly
be called the promise of honor, is for example,
the act of consecration made on entering into
some pious association; for, although certain
promises are made then, even with some solemnity, the conscience is not bound thereby, and
no obligation under pain of sin is contracted.

I speak of simple associations of piety; for
there are in the Church some associations constituted by it, such as the Congregation of St.
Sulpice, of the Oratory, etc., in which without
any vows being made, it could happen that a
promise of stability, would become an affair of
conscience, because a person would thereby have
bound himself to that extent to the body of
men with whom he desired to be associated.

But there is also towards God the promise of
contract, and that is the *vow*, which comes
then, as such, to impose by itself a new bond
on the conscience. We shall soon appreciate
the gravity of this promise made to God Himself. Let us say here only this that if there is

no intention of binding oneself under pain of
sin, there is no vow; and, indeed, if you be
not certain of your intention in promising,
your conscience is not bound by a doubtful obligation.

SECTION II.—*The Vow is a deliberate promise.*

By *a deliberate act* is understood one that presents these three essential conditions: knowledge of what we are doing, determination of the
will, and the power to do otherwise, if we so desired. It therefore belongs to the essence of the
vow that it should be an act entirely deliberate, for otherwise it would not exist.

I.—A vow requires the sufficient knowledge
of what is promised to God. It even calls for
mature consideration by the mind and a suitable appreciation; for as St. Thomas observes:
"It is an act of reason, to which belongs the
right to act with order."(1) This is why discretion is so necessary therein, that oftentimes
the advice of prudent persons should be sought
beforehand, because in treating with God levity
and blundering are equally out of place. Unfortunately this is not always thought of by
those who make vows.

But this condition becomes much more indispensable to the vows of religion, which are so
great an act of the free will and an engagement for the entire life. It is especially for
those vows that a clear and precise knowledge

(1) Votum est actus rationis, ad quam pertinet ordinare.
2a, 2æ, q. 88, a. 1.

of what is promised is required. Hence, it is the duty of superiors and masters of novices to fully instruct the aspirant to the religious life concerning it, to disguise nothing therein to him, not to seek to surprise him; an affair of this nature should not be treated of by stealth, through calculation of temporal interest or through human or earthly prudence; hence also it is the duty of the postulant and the novice to examine into the requirements of that state of life, to interrogate in his doubts, and to clearly know how things are.

If the person who makes the vows were ignorant of some point belonging to their substance or of some circumstance of such a nature, that if known to him, it would change his determination, his vows would be null through want of knowledge.

II.—The consent of the will is necessary for any vow, and for the vows of religion a very special consent is necessary, and this consent should be preceded by a trial of one's strength during at least one whole year. Not only is this a prescription of the Church, but even a condition made by it, without which the vows of religion would not be valid. (1)

This consent rests on a *first* and a *second probation*. The *first probation*, whether consisting of a certain number of days forming a part of the novitiate, or preceding it under the name of *postulate*, has for its object to make a first

(1) Council of Trent, Sess. 25, On Reform, c. 15.

examination, in order to know the vocation of God and to sound one's own heart. Therein one deliberates with oneself and with the superiors of the Order or of the Congregation; and the candidate should notice well that he must do his part in this deliberation, just as the Order is bound to do its.

The part of the candidate consists only in seeing *if he wills*, according to these words of Our Lord to the young man of the Gospel: "If thou wilt be perfect." (Matt. xix, 21), still as it is a question also of a vocation on the part of God, and as Our Lord also said: "You have not chosen me: but I have chosen you," (John xv, 16), the candidate for the religious life sounds his will to discover if God wills conjointly with himself and consequently if he himself wills rightly, that is by the impulse of God, Who is the principal cause of Man's good will. (*) The ordinary means for him to verify this capital point if by examining two things: the first, if he wills according to right reason, that is, without his purpose being a passing whim or a simple flight of the imagination, and without his overlooking some obligation of a nature to detain him by rights elsewhere; the second, if he wills purely and truly for God, not allowing himself to be influenced by human or defective motives.

Such should be the part of the candidate in which a director or superiors may be necessary

---

* For it is God who worketh in you, both to will and to accomplish, according to *His* good will. Philippians, ii, 13.

in order to help him by their lights and to keep illusions from him, but in which no one can supply the indecision of his will.

The part of the Order is to judge whether this same candidate is fitted to this vocation, and to pronounce definitively whether or not there is a true call from God: for, finally, grace could inspire a good desire, without always willing its execution, since the good desire is already a meritorious act and may become profitable to the soul in more than one respect. The superiors of the Order therefore examine the aptitudes of the subject relatively to their own institute: aptitudes of body as to health, strength, etc.; aptitudes of the mind as to uprightness and solidity, as to accomplishments acquired or dispositions to acquire them; aptitudes of the heart as to inclinations, habits and character. The candidate must understand that here the role of judge no longer belongs to him, because in wishing to render the verdict himself, he could fall into error, through ignorance or presumption or even through excess of diffidence. His only duty is to answer with candor the questions put to him, and honestly to make himself known.

The second probation, or *the novitiate*, by putting the candidate to the trial of the religious life and its difficulties, according to the institute, has as its end to confirm the choice of that state of life, the admission into the Order and the vocation as a whole. And in fact, this trial, provided that the novice gives himself to it with fidelity, will furnish a demonstration leaving no doubts; to the point that even had something been wanting to the work of the first probation, if the second proceed as it should, vainly shall the tempter come later on to strive to trouble the soul; rightfully, then, can the novice be told, whatever may have been the first deliberation: "Now you have knowingly persevered in this vocation when better known; you have sought therein God and your perfection; there, has been then, not only a ratification of the first act, but also a supplement to any defect therein to be found. The novice must remark that, his first probation once ended, it is his duty no longer to deliberate, as if he had always to fix his choice, since this indecision would paralyze all the effort of his will, but rather to undergo with courage the trials of the novitiate and to acquire the virtues and habits of the religious life, according to the institute to which God calls him.

III.—The act of the vow must be free and exempt from all constraint; but it is above all for the vows of religion that the most entire liberty is essential to him who pronounces them; otherwise the Church does not accept them and they remain without value. Not only would all pressure from without, such as threats, violence or dread cause the nullity of the act, but the same would be true of that fear which is called reverential, if it really hindered the liberty of the subject. The

Church watches over this point especially for the benefit of the timid sex and it has ordained that the Bishop shall ascertain by an examination the fullness of this liberty. (1)

SECTION III.—*The Vow is a promise made to God.*

"I will pay my vows to the Lord." (2) This is a very serious thought with which it is important to be well penetrated before making a vow, and no less important not to forget after having made it: the vow is a *promise* made to *God Himself.*

But assuredly when the vows of religion are concerned, this thought deserves the fullest consideration. Let us show that if it weighs on the soul, it also is apt to dilate it.

The vows of religion are, then, a strict engagement which man makes, and for life, towards God Himself; but we must add that reciprocal promises are made therein and that God on His side condescends to engage Himself towards men, so that the profession of these vows may be called a *synallagmatic contract* made between God and man. Therefore the religious may and should say to himself:

"I have made a contract with God, thence come my obligation, but God has also deigned to make a contract with me; hence my advantages."

I.—I have made a contract with God, I have made a promise to God Himself and not to

(1) Council of Trent, Sess. 25, On Reform, c. 17.
(2) I will pay my vows to the Lord. Psalm cxv.

men. Whence I must draw this first consequence; the accomplishment of my promise,
therefore, may in no wise depend upon the
conduct of men towards me. In vain would
I seek to give such efficacy to a wrong inflicted
on me by my superior, equals, or any one else,
as to believe myself dispensed from my promise made to God; the consideration of any
other than Himself can serve as no excuse and
be of no value.

I have made a promise to God and it is the
Almighty Who has taken notice of my obligation; He has entered it in His book, and no
one can efface it. He keeps it to produce it
some day, on that day on which He will make
me render an account of its execution. (1)

I have made a promise to God and He is the
All Seeing. He penetrates the darkness and
the depths of hearts: He sees the failings successfully hidden from the eyes of men; He
knows the whitened sepulchres which enclose
rottenness. Nothing can escape His eye,
neither the most secret recesses of the soul,
nor the least offences of unfaithfulness; and
He calls Himself the jealous God, Who exacts
all that has been promised to Him, and who
hates rapine in the holocaust.

I have made a promise to God and He is the
Immutable Being. Ah! this is the point to be
insisted on, for man is so inconstant. He is
as the leaf carried off by the wind, and what
he wills to-day, too often he wills it not to-

(1) Vow ye and pay to the Lord. Psalm lxxv.

morrow; and this inconstancy appears more common now than ever. Nevertheless when a promise has been made to God, it must be kept, and once engaged towards Him, it is done, the religious cannot retract. Apostasy! What a word! yet it is the correct word, the expression of the Church. Alas! some minds will yet go on imagining that they may change in this almost as one changes one's garments. You who have made a promise to God, you wish, because some unpleasantness has occurred, to go back. You have become disgusted with your holy state; at the least inconvenience you are heard to say: "If it is thus I shall get out." Hearken to Him Who has received your promise: "I am the Lord and I change not." (1) Hear the Prince of the Apostles: "Why hath Satan tempted thy heart, that thou shouldst lie to the Holy Ghost, and to keep back what no longer belongs to thee? Before engaging thyself, wast thou not free? Why hast thou conceived this thing in thy heart? Thou hast lied not to men but to God." (2) And we know what was the chastisement of Ananias and Sapphira.

(1) For I am the Lord and I change not. Malachias, iii, 6.
(2) Why hath Satan tempted thy heart that thou shouldst lie to the Holy Ghost and by fraud keep part of the price of the land? Whilst it remained did it not remain to thee? And after it was sold, was it not in thy power? Why hast thou conceived this thing in thy heart? Thou hast not lied to men but to God. And Ananias hearing these words fell down and gave up the ghost. Acts, v, 3, 4, 5.

However we do not speak here of what would be altogether a suggestion of the tempter: or, if we must speak of it, it is only to warn the religious of two things: The first of these is that in view of the gravity of this temptation it requires to be repulsed at its first onset, and that, if possible it should not even be listened to. The second of these is that the utmost care should be taken not to give rise through one's own fault to this temptation or to foment it by sadness, by wilful disgust, by susceptibilities or dislikes, by resistance to authority, by habitual violation of holy Rule. It is a most grievous thing wilfully to expose one's own fidelity, and among all the temptations that attack a religious none is more dangerous since none can cause him so great a harm.

Therefore no matter how short a time this temptation lasts, the religious is under obligation to make it known to whoever has the right to his confidences; this is often the only remedy for the evil and the most efficacious. Disclosing it to one's brethren is rigorously forbidden by charity: it would be a most blameworthy scandal as it would be like inoculating them with poison. Let us add further, that such confidences made to equals, even without an evil intention, almost always becomes hurtful to them; and besides, generally speaking, none of them has the grace to cure wounds of this kind. Finally, there is a serious duty of charity, for whosoever sees his brother in this peril—to notify the superior in order that he may hasten to his help.

Since we are considering so important a point, it behooves us to indicate the remedies to be resorted to by the persons themselves that are urged to unfaithfulness to their vocation by disgust of their state of life, by relaxation, or by the temptation of the enemy.

The first remedy is seriously to return to the consideration of God's right: "I have given myself, it is done, and hesitation is no longer lawful. To the repugnances of my evil nature, to the impulses of him who seeks to ruin me, I will reply by the energy of my will. I have, it is true, through my fault, allowed that energy to become weakened; but I am still free and master of myself, with God's help. Far from losing heart, as if it had become impossible for me to will now what I willed formerly, I shall rest on the infallible certitude of this double truth, that when God commands anything from me it is possible for me, and that He Himself Who imposes the duty is certainly present with His grace, if I only ask it, to help me to fulfill the obligation. (1)

A second remedy is the consideration of the chastisement which, ordinarily, even in this life, befalls the soul faithless to its promise. You feel the present suffering and your imagi-

(1) For God does not demand what is impossible, but when ordering warns you to do what you can and to seek what you cannot, and He will aid you in order that you can. Council of Trent, Sess. G., Ca. 10.

nation fails not still more to exaggerate it.
Pray, I might first say to you, only compare
it with the sufferings far heavier otherwise to
which the world condemns its own in positions
from which there is no escape. And, finally,
whatever may be your actual situation, are
you quite certain that your lot will be bettered
by unfaithfulness? Do you not know, on the
contrary, what is almost always shown by experience? And instead of profiting yourself
by these sad lessons, would you wish to add
one more example to them?

A third remedy, the sweetness of which will
be more efficacious, is the consideration of the
reciprocal promises made to you by God. But,
first, I wish to impart to you a precious secret
as a help, in general, in the difficulties to be
met in the service of God. This secret consists in never looking at things except on their
bright side. For every object in all the requirements of duty or virtue, presents two aspects
and, as it were, two faces. One frightens our
will, the other attracts it. Here, for example,
you experience repugnance, because you look
at the painful side, which presents the obligation or the difficulty; but rather make efforts
to see the agreeable aspect which shows you
a signal benefit of God, and your heart will
be strengthened thereby; esteem and gratitude
will be powerful aids in restoring the love of
vocation; prayer will do the rest.

II.—God has deigned to make a contract
with me.

In the promise given we have seen the obligation; but there is also the promise received; it is equally just to consider its profits and advantages. For to wish to consider in this contract only what weighs on us would be a pusillanimity both unreasonable, hurtful to us and offensive to God. Yes, doubtless, every honor obliges, every lucrative position or onerous contract imposes charges. But let us cast our eyes on worldlings themselves; do they obtain anything for nothing? Is it not true that they that pursue fortune or glory look more to the gain than the pain? "And for them," says the Apostle, "it is question only of a passing interest, whilst for us eternity is at stake." (1)

It is then true, that at the moment that I pledged my word to the Lord, He simultaneously engaged Himself to me.

God has made a contract with me: shall I ever be able to sufficiently understand the honor granted me thereby by the King of kings? Whilst so many others are only common servants, He has admitted me into His house that I might be in the ranks of His familiars; He has appointed me one of the officers of His palace; still more by this contract He has raised my soul to the dignity of spouse! Could it be possible for me to cease,

(1) And they indeed strive for the mastery that they may receive a corruptible crown; but we an incorruptible one. I Cor. ix, 25.

for a single day, to appreciate this honor and wish to correspond to it?

God, sovereignly faithful to His promises, has made a contract with me; whatever may be my weakness, I can count upon Him for the strength I need in my vocation. Whatever the difficulties; He shall always be at hand ready to sustain me; He Himself assures me of this by the mouth of an Apostle. (1)

God, the Almighty, has made a contract with me, and I have become His especial property by the complete gift that I have made to Him of my whole self. Now, when this Great God owns anything, He guards it, and there is no one strong enough to snatch it away from His Hands. (2)

God, the All-seeing, has made a contract with me; none of the least of my services will escape His notice, and all shall be faithfully, minutely counted. No good action, however small, no good intention, no good movement of my heart, no good desire even will be either forgotten or of no value in His sight.

God, the Immutable, has made a contract with me. Ah! this is the great cause of my confidence! For I need only to keep myself firmly attached to Him, and I thereby lose my natural instability. This was strongly felt by St. Paul, the Apostle: "I am sure," exclaimed he, with a marvellous assurance, "that

(1) God is faithful, by whom you are called. I Cor. i, 9.
(2) No man can snatch out of the hands of my Father. John, x, 29.

nothing can separate me from the love of my God." (1) And is this not for me too, wretched though I am, a truth proved by experience? This cupidity, this sensuality, this idolatry of one's own will, which so easily draw into disorders the poor souls who stay in the midst of the world and which have, perhaps, also formerly carried me away very far, what can they do against my heart now since it has attached itself to God and bound itself by this holy promise? This heart feels that it is free, it is steadfast notwithstanding its natural weakness, it struggles easily against inclinations thought to be indomitable by others, it contemns without effort or regret the goods, the honors, and the delights of the world; finally it is so faithful to duty that entire years often pass by without a single fault of any gravity to deplore. Whence these prodigies! It is God who with His mighty Hand upholds His frail creature. "He has promised it, he has done it says the prophet." (2) For this reason, rightly can I ever exclaim with David: "Yes, truly it is good for me to stick close to my God." (3)

(1) For I am sure that neither death, nor life, nor angels, nor principalities, nor powers, nor things present, nor things to come, nor might, nor height, nor depth, nor any other creature, shall be able to separate us from the love of God. Romans, viii, 38, 39.

(2) I the Lord have spoken and have done it. Ezech. xvii, 24.

(3) It is good for me to stick close to my God. Ps. lxxii.

Finally God, the infinitely rich and liberal
Master, has made a contract with me. Men
may have thought that I gave Him much by
my sacrifice, but whatsoever I had to offer
Him, what in reality was it for such a Lord
and in comparison with what He wished to
render to me? Ah! It is here, as says St.
Paul, that we must remember the words of
the Lord Jesus Himself declaring that it is
better to give than to receive. (1) When a
great king accepts a present it is because He
Himself wishes to give; he bestows an honor
first, by the very fact of having deigned to
accept and he afterwards adds those returns of
royal magnificence which he measures according to his dignity. When it is to God we
give, we at once receive His Love in exchange,
as the Apostle teaches: "God loveth a cheer-
ful giver;" (2) and the love of God, besides
its own value which is above all other trea-
sures, becomes the source of all goods, since
the Being infinitely rich cannot love any one
without wishing to enrich him. The liberality
of Our God awaits only ours towards Him to
satisfy its infinite need of pouring itself out
upon us. If then, in the promise I have made
to Him, I have offered all that I had and all
that I was, He on His side, has engaged Himself to give me with a hundredfold in this

(1) You ought to remember the words of the Lord Jesus,
how He said, "It is a more blessed thing to give rather
than to receive." Acts xx, 35.
(2) II Cor. ix, 7.

world and the abundance of His graces, that treasure in Heaven which is no other than Himself, the Ocean of all joys and all felicities. (1)

SECTION IV.—*The vow is the promise of a better act.*

We do not expatiate on these last words of the definition as they seem to us to have been sufficiently explained in the catechism itself. (2)

ARTICLE II.

THE VOW IS AN ACT OF THE VIRTUE OF RELIGION.

This truth is only affirmed by the catechism: touching reflections will be furnished to religious persons by its development.

SECTION I.—*The Vow belongs to Sacrifice.*

The excellence of the vow is evident from the fact that it is an act of the worship of latria, which is rendered only to God, in order to recognize His sovereign dominion and infinite greatness.

A promise can be made to the Blessed Virgin or to some Saint, but this promise will not, correctly speaking, be a vow, unless we bind ourselves for the honor of God, that is by assuming obligations towards Him under pain of sin. And it is precisely in this that the

(1) I am . . . thy reward exceeding great. Genesis, xv, 1.
(2) 1st Part, C. 1.

vows form a part of sacrifice, for there is then an immolation offered to God by the change effected in the object offered, in that it becomes by obligation a thing belonging to God.

The vow is a special participation in the sacrifice of Jesus Christ, by pronouncing and executing it we do what St. Paul says: "We fill up what is wanting of the Passion of the Saviour in our flesh;" (1) that is, we add the part that He reserved to us, to make us merit the application of His Divine Sacrifice. It is thus that at Mass, the bloody Sacrifice of Calvary is to be applied to men, by the unbloody sacrifice of the altar: because Mass is, at one and the same time, the oblation of the natural Body of Jesus Christ, and that of His mystical body which is the Christians: so that the immolation of the Head is profitable especially to those members who are careful to offer themselves together with Him. This immolation of the members is nowhere so conspicuous as in martyrdom and in the sacrifice made by the vows of religion. Whence is seen that religious have a manner of their own of celebrating or hearing Holy Mass, that of offering themselves as victims with Jesus Christ, by renewing the holocaust of their vows.

SECTION II.—*Of the Virtue of Religion.*

Religion, as is indicated by the very words, is the great virtue of a religious; at the moment

(1) I fill up those things that are wanting of the sufferings of Christ in my flesh. Coloss. i, 24.

he pronounces his vows, it becomes the special
virtue of his state. Hence the importance to
him of thoroughly knowing both what it is
and all concerning it. In order to instruct
him more thoroughly about it, we are going to
give an exposition of the beautiful teaching
of St. Thomas on this virtue. (1)

§ I.

Religion, says the holy doctor, is a virtue
forming a part of justice, and even its principal part, it is the one by which man renders to
God the worship and the homage that he owes
Him.

Let us insist on these two fundamental
thoughts, they are most worthy of consideration by religious:

. I.—Religion is a part of justice, for it belongs
to justice to render to each one his due; and it
is its principal part, for the first of our debts
is without doubt that which places us under
obligation to our Creator and God.

Let us, then, represent to ourselves this
Being and Supreme Lord, casting down His
looks from the height of Heaven over the sur-
face of the earth. He perceives three very distinct classes of men.

The first, alas! is composed of those who
disown, forget and offend Him: innumerable
class of intelligent creatures, who by refusing
to give to their Author the worship and the

_____

(1) 2a, 2æ, q. 81, a. 1.

homage due to Him, violate the most essential duties of justice.

The second class contains those, who, it is true, recognize Him for their Lord and do not deny His rights over them. But how rare is the resemblance of God among these men, all given over to their earthly interests! How small a place does the care of paying their debt to Him occupy in their life! That great God, Who should be all in all to them, sees but few acts of homage coming to Him from them! And in proportion as the intervals are great, so are the hearts rapacious and cold! Lowest of worship, which is too often only a formality, and in which those who render it do not even reach the indispensable nor the strict obligation of justice!

The third class presents to the Divine looks the persons who are truly religious: they are those who penetrated with the end of their creation, and drawing the just consequences from the fundamental truth, place at the head of their obligations those which refer to the Creation. In the first rank should doubtless be found those who are called *religious*, for *they have entered religion*, that is, they have destined themselves by their very state, to verify in themselves in an excellent manner the definition of the virtue of religion; and when they are such in fact, as their name and profession imply, it is on them, assuredly that the eyes of the Lord rest with the greatest complacency, according to what He Himself said of the holy place in which religion is especially attended to: "My eyes and my heart shall be there always." (1)

II.—The virtue of religion renders to God the worship and the homage that are due to Him. But in what does this worship and homage consist? The angelic doctor gives a double etymology impressing on the mind two fruitful ideas, whence he draws the substantial idea of religion. The word *religion*, he says, comes from the Latin verb *religare, to bind again*; or again from the verb *reeligere, to re-elect, or choose anew.* Thus religion binds us again to Almighty God from whom we had become detached. It again makes us re-elect God, whom we had lost through negligence, that is, according to the strength of the word *negligere, nec eligere,* because our heart no longer wished for Him. In fact, God is He to whom man should principally re-bind himself as being his supreme and inseparable first beginning; and He is likewise, He towards whom man should bring back his wandering heart as towards his last end; so that he may regain by faith operating in good works, the God whom he had lost through negligence. (2)

This is essentially the twofold idea of the worship that we owe to God, and this doctrine

(1) III Kings, ix, 3.

(2) Religio from re-binding, because it binds us again to the omnipotent God; religion from a choosing anew, because we choose Him again whom we had lost through neglect.

on religion reaches out to all mankind. Man naturally bound to God, His Creator by his origin, was still more so, supernaturally, by grace, with which he had been adorned; but Adam's sin had unfortunately detached him from God, and a Repairer had to come to bind him again to his first beginning. In consequence of the same sin, the human will, no longer caring for God, took elsewhere its guilty choice; a Saviour was necessary to cure this will and render it capable of re-electing Him who is its last end. Still too often detached by new sins which cause him to lose God, he must make fresh efforts, with the help of the ever-merciful grace of Jesus Christ, to bind himself again to his first beginning and to bring back his will to his last end. This must be the continual work, the daily care of man on earth, and it belongs to religion to accomplish it. To have religion, to practice one's religion means nothing else.

But this universal principle, common to all, has for the religious a very special application; for it is the proper expression of all his duties, and it urges him to fulfil them by these two supreme motives, God, my first beginning, God my last end. God, my first beginning, to Whom I must ever more strongly and more entirely bind myself; God, my last end Whom my heart must ceaselessly re-elect with more efficacy. What efforts must not the religious make in order to attain this! How many voids to fill up! How many things to repair every day! How many adverse inclinations to be

combatted!   And this is the very reason of the
multiplicity of means offered by the religious
profession :—the vows, the rules, the spiritual
exercises, direction by superiors—all having for
their object to aid one to bind one's self more
perfectly to one's first beginning and to re-
elect always more energetically one's last end.

III.—Let us now consider more clearly the
composition of that debt to the Lord which
religion must pay.

First, man owes God the worship of latria
which is due to Him only.   Then obedience is.
due to God in all that He exacts by a formal
precept which excludes all sin, whether grievous
or slight.   But in the third place we moreover owe Him all we are capable of doing for
His service and glory, even though He command it not under pain of sin: because all our
works are His due as Creator and Lord, Beginning and End, and because we are in every way
His servants.   It is true, that the works not
rigorously commanded by Him, are called *supererogatory.*   But there can be in fact on our
part, relatively to the exigencies of His Greatness, no act of pure liberality; far from that,
we shall never have paid our entire debt no matter what we may do; and we shall ever have to
say in presence of this Divine Master: "We
are useless servants; we have done only what
was our duty to do." (1)   Thence the name
of *just* given to all His servants; for even

(1) Say: We are unprofitable servants—we have done
that which we ought to do. Luke, xvii, 10.

whilst performing heroic works in His honor, they do only what is in accordance with justice.

Now, must we ask the religious if there be any one on earth more justly and more totally bound by obligation to God than he is? But we must also add: Is there any one else in so favorable a position to be able to pay easily all the parts of his debt?

§ II.

Another teaching of St. Thomas, on the virtue of religion contains the practical manner of discharging this debt, and we shall there see three things: 1st, the religious life in all its details; 2nd, the essence of the religious spirit; 3rd, the true exercise of religion. (1)

I.—The virtue of religion, says the holy doctor, produces two kinds of acts: those of its own, which it brings forth formally, and those that it commands to the other virtues in order that it may take them to itself by referring them to its last end, and they give them more value.

Among the acts peculiar to religion, some are interior, others exterior.

These interior acts embrace the principal cultus that we owe to God. The first of these acts and the one that gives activity to all the others is *devotion;* for devotion is nothing but promptitude of the will to go at

(1) 2a, 2æ, q. 81, a. 2.

everything that belongs to God's honor and service. The second of these acts is *prayer*, by which man honors God and submits himself to Him, as in praying he professes that he has need of God as the author of all good.

The exterior acts of religion are adoration, sacrifice, offerings, praise, etc. An explanation of these matters would no doubt be useful; but it would overload the present question and lead us too far: but on account of its importance, we, shall, further on, return to devotion. (1)

Numberless are the acts which religion can command to the other virtues: for all enter into its domain and acquire its especial merit from the very fact that it refers them to the worship and the honor of God. Such are the works of mercy, of temperance and of mortification, according to what St. James says: "Religion clean and undefiled, before God and the Father is this: to visit the fatherless and widows in their tribulation: and to keep one's self unspotted from this world." (2)

The same is true of the acts that proceed from some legitimate affection inspired by nature, as the love of relatives and friends, the study of science, the taste for such or such an honest occupation, etc. Religion does not suppress these affections; it purifies them, frees them from selfish and worldly love, strengthens and perfects them by referring them to God; and thus it makes of them holy

(1) Section III.   (2) St. James' Epistle, i, 27.

affections, having God Himself as their beginning and end.

Even the most indifferent and most common actions can thus be made its own by religion, as the Apostle Paul teaches and urges us: "Therefore whether you eat or drink, or whatsoever else you do; do all for the glory of God." (1)

We have here then, all the details of the religious life. We see that not only can a religious, like other Christians, transform all that he does into acts of religion by the intention animating him; but moreover, that his vows, above all that of obedience, are there to confer upon his works a much more special merit of religion and to refer all in an excellent manner to the worship of the Divine Master.

II.—Now the very essence of the religious spirit, which should penetrate all our actions, is this: By the virtue of religion, again says St. Thomas, man reveres and honors God as first principle as well for the creation as for the government of all things, especially of man himself. This is why the Lord said by His prophet: "If then I be a father, where is my honor?" (2) For it belongs to a father to communicate existence to his children and to govern them. (3)

Let us comprehend thoroughly the bearing of this doctrine. The religious spirit essentially consists in ever seeing in God the first

(1) I Cor. x, 31. (2) Malachias, i, 6.
(3) 2a, 2æ, quæst. 81, art. 3.

Principle in order always to honor Him faithfully in this quality. But where does God manifest Himself as first Principle? In the creation and the government of the world and all things. The religious spirit, then, renders man everywhere attentive to recognize this divine action and diligent to render Him homage. However there is one special place wherein his attention and diligence should be greater still and more continual: his own person; and it is in himself above all that he loves to consider God as first Principle in order to honor Him who in the natural and the supernatural order, with the authority and goodness of a Father, produces, preserves, and governs, His reasonable creature.

Doubtless, such was the religious spirit from the origin of the world; men truly religious, even among that people among whom the law of fear prevailed on account of the hardness of their hearts, knew how to recognize that quality of Father in the God of majesty. But Jesus Christ came to mark religion with this character more openly, whom associating those who believe in Him to His own filiation, "He gave them the power to be made the sons of God." (1)

In whom should that filial cultus, in which the Holy Ghost Himself causes us to exclaim, "Father, Father," (2) when we treat with the

(1) John, i, 12.
(2) You have received the Spirit of adoption of sons, whereby we cry Abba (Father). Romans, viii, 15.

Creator, reign more than in the mind and heart of the religious towards the celestial Father? In reading the lives of the Saints, for example that of St. Teresa, we are struck with the manner in which they knew how to unite the most profound respect for God, with the most tender love. Ah! it is only in the relations of men among themselves that familiarity breeds contempt, or that respect constrains the effusion of love. But it is quite otherwise with God, because the Holy Ghost is present to producing at the same time the profound sentiment of majesty and bounty.

III. — Here, finally, is according to St. Thomas, the true exercise of religion, such as is necessary without doubt for all Christians, but such as the religious most of all should have in all the relations of his life. The virtue of religion, says that saint, honors and serves God by the same acts: for the worship refers to the Divine excellence to Whom reverence is due, and the service refers to the dependence of man who by his natural condition is obliged to render homage to God. These two things, worship and service, are necessarily found in all the acts belonging to religion, because all should be the testimonies by which man declares at the same time the Divine Excellence and his own dependence, whether he offers something to God, such as adoration, praise, sacrifice, etc., or in his turn asks or receives some benefit from the Divine Bounty. (1)

(1) 2a, 2æ, quæst. 81, art. 3.

Who does not see how fundamental this is in the Christian and religious life. These two things, honoring and serving God, are never to be separated in the true and solid practice of the virtue of religion: for, if He asks and welcomes the protestations that we make of His Excellence, He no less requires the submission of our will and the service of our works.

§ III.

The virtue of religion is not a theological virtue, because God is not its immediate object as He is of faith, hope and charity. The object of religion is not our last end, but all the acts which serve as means to attain it.

It is therefore only a moral virtue; but it is the first of all in dignity, for the reason that it approaches nearest to God and that it is closest to our last end, operating works directly tending to the Divine glory.

Nevertheless St. Augustine teaches us that man honors God by faith, hope and charity; (1) because these virtues by themselves commanding religion to act, cause these acts to become their own also. This is a principle most carefully to be remembered, as it is most fruitful in practical consequences. We there see that the more are faith, hope and charity living in a soul, the more do they cause religion to produce therein works pertaining to the worship and the service of God. On the

(1) Fide, spe et charitate colitur Deus. God is worshipped by faith, hope and charity.

contrary, in proportion as they decrease, so does the virtue of religion become inactive, even so far as to fall into complete desuetude.

§ IV.

The preceding exposition of the virtue of religion brings vividly into view the excellence of the religious state. Therefore St. Thomas, explaining to religious the meaning of the name they bear, herein finds the reason why this appellation is so specially attributed to them.

The name religious, he says, is by antonomasia given to those who have devoted themselves entirely to the service of God, because they are men who, among other men, offer that perfect sacrifice of holocaust, in which is reserved no portion of the victim. (1) Therefore religious, by their very state, are and should be the personification of the virtue of religion, the virtue of religion ever in action. This is their essential obligation, but it also is their special merit and the beautiful portion given them by God: so that every one of them should continually apply to himself the words addressed by St. Leo, to the Christian: "Understand thy dignity, O religious, and after having been so elevated by the Divine Master in His service, do not lower thyself by thy works nor return to the pitiful meanness and futility of worldly

(1) Antonomastice religiosi dicuntur illi qui se totaliter mancipant divino servitio, quasi holocaustum Deo offerentes. 2a, 2æ, q. 186, a. 1.

life." (1) The name religious is, every time it
is pronounced, a call to fervor to him who bears
it a call like unto that made to himself by St.
Bernard: "Bernard, for what purpose camest
thou hither?" This name is like a spiritual
mirror perpetually before the eyes of the religious: let him interrogate and consult it and
he will see it ever repeating the great lesson
given to men by the Child-God in His first public act of religion: "I must be about my
Father's business." (2)

SECTION III.—*On Devotion.*

Devotion is the first and principal act of the
virtue of religion, as we have already said: for
it is by it that the will is borne to all the
others, either to those produced by this virtue itself, whether within or without, or to
those it causes the others to produce in order
that God may be honored.

There are two kinds of devotion to be distinguished: substantial and accidental devotion.

§ I.—*Substantial devotion.* (3)

I.—*Devotion,* considered in its substance, is
nothing else but a certain promptitude of the
will giving itself to all that belongs to the
service of God. (4)

(1) Agnosce, O Christiane, dignitatem tuam, et divinae
consors factus naturæ, noli in veterem vilitatem degeneri
conversatione redire.

(2) Luke, ii, 49.　　　　(3) 2a, 2æ, q. 82, a. 1, 2.

(4) Devotio nihil aliud est quam voluntas quaedam
prompte se tradendi ad ea quae sunt Dei famulatus.

The word devotion comes from the Latin *devovere*, and *devoti* was the term applied by the Romans to those who devoted themselves to their gods and to death for their country; as, according to Titus Livy, was done by the two Decius. To be *devout*, therefore, is to give up with a prompt will one's life with its acts to the worship and the service of God; and devotion is not, as many imagine it to be, an affair of sensibility, but one of *devotedness*. It does not consist precisely in pious practices, but in the ardor of a will which goes at the things which are asked of it by God.

St. Francis de Sales has spoken of devotion in the same manner as the Angelic Doctor: "It is nothing else," he tells us, "but a spiritual agility and vivacity which makes us labor for God carefully, frequently and promptly."

II.—The special and direct *enemy of devotion* is *spiritual sloth* or *tepidity*. (1)

The vice of sloth is, as a rule, a sadness which weighs on the soul when in presence of good to be done, and so depresses the courage of a person that he no longer has will to act. Sloth has two vicious sides: it is, first, vicious in itself because it treats as evil what is good: for sadness is that sentiment of the soul that strives against evil to repulse it. Secondly, Sloth is perverse in its effects, because it prevents the doing of good. Moreover, as no one

(1) 2a, 2æ, q. 35, a. 1. Acedia est quaedam tristitia aggravans, quae scilicet ita deprimit animum hominis ut nihil agere libeat.

can remain under the pressure of sadness nor live without some contentment, sloth causes the soul to seek sensual satisfactions. Finally after having turned away from the good which saddened it, the will becomes so perverted, as even to oppose that good either in things by an aversion of malice or in persons by hatred of those whose advice or whose example recalls it to its duty.

Apply all this to spiritual sloth, which is the *wilful* disgust of the soul for works pertaining to the service of God and you have well characterized the terrible evil of tepidity and its effects. But it is to be remarked, that here nothing is said of involuntary disgusts when in spite of them the will remains faithful to the practice of its duties.

III.—*The causes of devotion* show how it can be enkindled in the heart. *Charity* is its *proximate cause* and its *remote cause* is *contemplation.* (1)

Charity is the proximate cause of devotion, because it belongs to love to. make a friend prompt to render service to his friend. And it is God who gives to us and augments in us charity: from Him therefore, must we ask the cause, if we wish to possess the effect.

Nevertheless, on the other hand, charity is itself fed by devotion, as every friendship is preserved and increased by the exercise of the works which it produces. And this is the share we must contribute to nourish holy love

(1) 2a, 2æ, q. 82, a. 3, 4, 6.

within ourselves. Let us also listen to St.
Francis de Sales: "By means of this spiritual
agility and vivacity of our will, charity acts
within us, or we through it, promptly and lovingly. Charity is a spiritual fire, and devotion
adds the flame thereunto which renders charity
prompt, active and diligent."

Contemplation is the remote cause of devotion, that is, meditation and spiritual reading
especially, because it is thus that the soul con-
ceives the will to give itself with promptitude
to the service of God. In fact, every act of
our will proceeds from some consideration of
our understanding; and devotion rises in us
from a double consideration: one wherein we
contemplate the Divine Goodness, the other
which shows us our own misery. The contemplation of the Divine Goodness excites in us
the love of it, which is, as we have said, the
proximate cause of devotion, according to
these words of the Psalmist: "It is good for
me to stick close to my God, to put my hope
in the Lord." (1) The consideration of the
Divine attributes in themselves, *is of itself* the
best means of exciting devotion. But *on our
side*, on account of human weakness, the most
efficacious consideration to this end is that of
Our Lord Jesus Christ, God made man like us
and for us, of Jesus Christ Who has appeared to
us as being the grace, the benignity and the
humanity of Our Saviour. (2) This is the

(1) Psalm lxxii, 28.
(2) Apparuit Dei gratia Salvatoris nostri.—Tit. 2. Benig-
nitas et humanitas apparuit Salvatoris nostri Dei.—Tit. 2.

book written within and without (1) which it behooves us to read and meditate, after St. Paul's example, who after having been taken up to the third heaven, professed to know nothing but Jesus and Jesus Crucified. (2)

The other source of devotion is the consideration of our misery. For the more we shall be penetrated with it the more will it make us feel our need of leaning on God, and consequently the more shall we strive to merit His help by the fidelity of our services, according to these words of David: "I have lifted up my eyes to the holy mountains whence help shall come to me, the help of Him who made Heaven and earth." (3) Moreover, this view of our misery will exclude presumption, which prevents man, because he leans on his own strength from subjecting himself to God.

All that has been said shows how necessary is meditation and why it is called an *exercise of devotion*. Made with diligence it serves to inflame devotion, but if made without care and for form-sake it lets it become extinguished.

IV.—*The effects of devotion.* Principally and directly devotion produces joy; but it also, indirectly, produces a certain sadness according to God.

(2) And I saw in the right hand of him that sat on the throne a book written within and without. Apoc. v, 1.

(3) For I judged not myself to know anything among you but Jesus Christ and Him crucified. I Cor. ii, 2.

(1) Psalm cxx, 1, 2.

In fact, the consideration of the Divine
Goodness, which is, as we have seen is the
cause of devotion, of itself produces joyfulness
in the soul: "I remembered God and I was
delighted," (1) says the holy King David.
Worldlings imagine that devotion is sad and
gloomy, that is because they do not know how
far above earthly joys and pleasures, is the content of a heart which is entirely God's. Or
they consider only those who drag themselves
along painfully in God's service instead of
putting forth in it that promptitude of a will
which knows how to give cheerfully to the
Lord. But let them cast their eyes on those
who possess true devotion, and in every instance shall they find hearts contented with
God, because those hearts in all things apply
themselves to please Him. This is the example offered by all the Saints: St. Romuald who
served the Divine Master with so much ardor
for more than a hundred years, always had so
radiant a countenance as to communicate his
joy to those who looked upon him, (2) and the
amiability of St. Francis Xavier was such
that a Pagan King of Japan because of it conceived the desire to go to Heaven in order to
be in his company. (3) Like the Saints, every
true servant of God can and should give this
edification to the world.

(1) Psalm lxxvi, 4.
(2) Vultu adeo læto semper erat, ut intuentes exhilara·
ret. (Lit.)
(3) History of his life.

Yet this very consideration of the Divine Goodness indirectly causes a certain sadness in the devout soul, the sadness of the exile repeating with the Psalmist: "My soul hath thirsted after the strong living God; when shall I come and appear before the face of God? My tears have been my bread day and night." (1) But this very sadness is one of the beatitudes here below: "Blessed are they that mourn; for they shall be comforted." (2)

Doubtless the devout soul draws a subject of sadness from the consideration of its own misery, but it draws also therefrom a subject of joy, from the thought that the misery felt and humbly acknowledged by us, infallibly draws down mercy. And this element of joy is necessary to the comforting of those who mourn, because without it the sight of our misery would produce only dejection with a melancholy that would not be according to God.

Whence it follows that wilful anxieties in God's service, are not good indications of real devotion, since it does not join to the sentiment of its evils the assurance of being succored.

V.—When substantial devotion is a habit in the soul it is properly called *fervor of spirit*, it proceeds from charity and in its turn serves to nourish it, as said above; but this true fervor is essential, just as charity is in the will, and not in sensible impressions.

(1) Psalm xli, 3, 4.   (2) Matt. v, 5.

§ 2.—*Accidental Devotion.*

I.—A certain sweetness experienced by the soul, supporting the promptitude of its will in what it does for God, is what is termed *accidental devotion.* It is only an *accident* overadded to devotion and not its very substance: so that devotion can well exist without it.

II.—There may be two kinds of suavity felt in devotion: either it charms only the will, or this sweetness affects the sensibility of the soul, and, as it is termed, the inferior appetite.

The first species of suavity is a joy purely spiritual. Generally speaking, even in the suffering of sacrifice, man always finds a content of mind, which is as the natural reward of the will when it is prompt in its act of virtue. But it often happens that this content remains latent as it were, in the depth of the soul, for example, as when the will has to make an effort against sensible pain or the difficulty of the work. In order that the suavity may become intense and perceptible, the unction of God's grace must be added, and this is the first kind of accidental devotion, which makes the will experience a profound joy, in which the inferior sensibility takes no part, it is like unto the delights experienced by the angelic spirits.

This wholly spiritual sweetness is what St. Francis de Sales seems to have wished to describe in the following graceful passage: "Devotion is the sweetness of sweetnesses and

the queen of virtues: for it is the perfection
of charity. If charity is a milk, devotion is
the cream; if it is a plant, devotion is the
fruit; if it is a precious stone, devotion is its
brilliancy; if it is a balm, devotion is its fragrance, the fragrance of suavity comforting men
and rejoicing the angels." It had also been
said by St. Bernard in fewer words, but with
no less grace, that devotion is a flower of the
future world: *ævi futuri flos est devotio*.

But another trait may be presented by the
suavity of accidental devotion: namely, when
certain pleasant emotions are produced in the
sensible or inferior part of the soul, and then
it may properly be called *sensible devotion*.

If to these sweet emotions of sentiment
be joined true devotedness of the will, then
it is the devotion real; but if devotedness in
works does not exist with the sensible impres-
sion, the devotion is only apparent and illusory.
Sensible devotion is therefore to be judged by
its fruits and not by sentiment.

It may not only be a vain appearance, but
even a deceit of the evil spirit or of self-love,
and consequently an enemy of true devotion;
whence we see how important is the examination of its origin.

The sensible sweetness of devotion may have
the four following causes:

1st. The intensity of the act of charity; for
says St. Thomas (1) so great a satisfaction may

(1) Propter intensionem appetitus superioris, ex quo fit
redundantia in inferiorem partem. 1a, 2æ, q. 30, art. 5.

be produced by the intensity of an act of the will, as to cause its superabundance to overflow and react on the inferior part of the soul. This may, above all, take place in the intense act of charity, when God adds to it the unction of a special grace: then are sensible emotions produced, tears and other effects more or less vehement, as are read in the lives of the Saints; so that one may exclaim with the Psalmist: "My heart and my flesh have rejoiced in the living God." (1)

2nd. The action of the good angel. In fact, it often happens, that when the soul does or wishes to do something for God's service, the good angel approaches to lend it his aid, and by an action belonging to the natural power of angels, (2) he excites in the inferior part of the soul emotions whence proceed the sensible sweetnesses of devotion. His purpose is to second the will in good by furnishing it this agreeable help, this rampart against the repugnances of the flesh.

3rd. But the wicked angel on his side possesses naturally the power to excite in us emotions and sensible sweetnesses, which may be mistaken for devotion, and he does excite them without any good being done by us or without its being done for God. His purpose is always to do us harm by this deceitful enticement and thus artfully to prepare our ruin.

(2) Psalm lxxxiii, 3.
(3) See St. Thomas, Part 1st, quest. III.

4th. Finally, in certain impressionable natures self-love by itself can likewise successfully produce a seeming devotion with its sensible effects; this fruit of self-love cannot be good, even if it causes good actions, since the intention spoils them and these lying sweetnesses serve only to lead the soul farther and farther astray out of the path of the true service of God.

To sum up, then, there is a purely spiritual sweetness, which, as St. Paul, tells us, is entirely above the senses; though more rarely felt by souls of ordinary devotion, it is frequent among the Saints, who even here below, according to St. Denis (1) share on account of their superabundant charity, the delights of the angels. As to the delights of sensible devotion, they may be indications of an ardent charity; but these indications are far from being infallible: for on one side, a manly temperament may naturally be less open to sensible impressions, even in the most intense acts of the will, although it must be acknowledged that God has often given to great souls hearts full of tenderness. On the other hand, sensible consolations may be the indications of a lesser charity, because it is to persons of weak or unstable will that the good spirit is wont to lend support in this manner, and he gives it even to souls without charity in order to draw them to

(1) Sancti homines multoties fiunt in communicatione delectationum angelicarum. Many holy persons participate in the delights of the angels.

God. Finally, they may be deceiving indications of charity as when they are the work of the devil or of self-love.

The practical conclusion of all this is, that we should cling above all to substantial devotion.

Is it not, however, lawful to desire and to seek sensible devotion?

In the first place, I answer by quoting a proposition condemned by the Church in Molinos, the false mystic of the XVII century: "He who desires and seizes sensible devotion, does wrong in wishing and striving for it." (1) The contrary proposition is therefore true: He does not do wrong. And, in fact, sensible devotion is a gift from God; for that reason it should be esteemed, and should He deign to grant it, it ought to be received with gratitude. It may be a necessary stay to our weakness to support us in well-doing; it is therefore to be asked for with humble sentiments of the need we may have of it. It is very useful to make us advance in all virtues; we should then desire it, strive to merit it by mortification and purity of life, and whenever given to us by God, faithfully use it as an instrument of spiritual progress.

I answer, in the second place, that as it is possible for sensible devotion to be false, care should be taken to discover as I have said whence

(1) Qui desiderat et amplectitur devotionem sensibilem, male facit eam desiderando et ad eam conando. Condemned Proposition.

it proceeds. Moreover, even when the good spirit is the source of it, it is one of the favors that can be used either for good or for evil. He abuses it who instead of availing himself of it to gather strength and to prepare with it for the time of trial, thinks only of enjoying it for itself. This is what St. John of the Cross calls *spiritual sensuality*, by which we cling improperly to the gift rather than to the giver. It is therefore a grace for those sensual souls when God withdraws consolation from them, just as the physician prescribes a diet to cure a malady caused by gluttony. Finally let us be sure that we are not rendered agreeable to God by sensible relish. Far from that, it often happens that we are all the less pleasing to Him when we are most pleased with ourselves and when we congratulate ourselves, because, as we think, things are going on so well. But let us not deceive ourselves, humility and the conviction of our misery, the promptitude of our will in doing His in all things, the care to practice solid virtue, whether He gives us much or little spiritual consolations, these are the things that please Our Divine Master.

SECTION IV.—*Religion compared with Sanctity.*(1)

We willingly add here this consideration, which is of great interest to every Christian and especially to persons in religion.

(1) 2a, 2æ, q. 81, a. 3.

I.—What is sanctity?

An ardent and generous heart easily causes him who embraces the religious state to say: "I wish to become a saint herein." On the contrary, it may often happen that a pusillanimous religious will be heard to say to himself and to repeat to others: "As for me I have no pretension of becoming a saint, it would be too high an aim for my weakness." Well! the Angelic Doctor will answer to the first that to be a saint he has only to be a true religious; but the second will also learn from him that not to wish to become a saint is to give up the purpose of being a true religious; that is, not to desire to be what is meant by his very name, and in such a case there will remain to him only the appearance, the bark, the mask of religion.

In fact, St. Thomas tells us that the difference between religion and sanctity is only a *difference of reason*, that is, a difference in the aspects under which our mind considers them; but that at bottom, their essence is the same: for the part of religion is to render to God the worship that is due to Him, by referring its own acts and those it causes the other virtues to produce to the divine honor, and *sanctity consists precisely in this that the soul applies itself and all its acts to God.* (1)

Thence we manifestly see, that both definitively do an identical work: religion in order

(1) Sanctitas dicitur, per quam mens hominis seipsam et suos actus applicat Deo.

to pay the debt resting on us towards the Supreme Majesty; Sanctity to make our soul reach its perfection by applying it to the Infinitely perfect Being. And this is also the work that is done by charity, under this other aspect that it unites us to God by our heart and stamps the acts of all our other virtues with the seal of divine love.

It should, moreover, be remarked, that as there are in the practice of religion and of charity two different degrees, one indispensable to salvation, the other rising higher, thus we should distinguish two kinds of sanctity: one without which Heaven is not to be hoped for, the other which does not stop at this inferior degree. Doubtless it may be said to ordinary Christians themselves, that to be satisfied through a feeling of cowardice and as if by a set plan, to aim only at the inferior degree, is to putting one's salvation in great peril, because if it be missed, there is some below it, and to miss it in reality is but too easy to our weakness, if we aim not at the very least a little higher. But whatever may be the case of Christians in the world, we shall soon see, when speaking of the obligation of religious to tending to perfection, that it is not permitted him to be satisfied with an ordinary charity nor with an ordinary sanctity, just as his name warns him that ordinary religion cannot be sufficient for him.

II.—St. Thomas shall now set forth the two elements of sanctity with very clear and precise notions. The name sanctity, he says, contains two things, the first is cleanness, or exemption from stain, which allows the soul to apply itself to God; the second is firmness or a certain strength in the tie which binds it to God. (1)

1st. In order that the soul may be in a condition to apply itself to God with its acts, it must first be pure, according to these words of the Apostle: "What fellowship hath light with darkness?" (2) The soul is soiled by applying itself to objects below it; for every substance is corrupted by its mixture with an inferior one: gold, for example, ceases to be pure when mixed with lead. The soul then must be disengaged from the low things which soil it in order to be able to apply itself to the supreme object, God.

The Greek tongue has given us the word that expresses this first element of sanctity: *Agios, ·sine terra*, not soiled by contact with the earth. Thus pure water looks like beautiful crystal; a drop penetrated by light is like a diamond; mixed with earth, it is only mud.

This part of sanctity, as is seen, embraces all that relates to detachment and to abnegation, and we shall not enter here into details. Let us say only that nothing is more useful to excite us to this purity of soul, than to consider it frequently in the saints. How care-

(1) Nomen sanctitatis videtur duo importere: numditiam et firmitatem.

(2) II Cor. vi, 14.

fully did not St. John the Baptist, St. Aloysius Gonzaga, and so many pure virgins avoid all contact with terrestrial things! Prayer and good will can make us approach the saints by imitation; and the souls that sincerely give themselves up to the spirit of grace will feel that past ages have not exhausted the source of sanctity and that the arm of God has not been shortened.

2ndly. The Latin language has given us the word that expresses the second element of sanctity: *Sanctus*, that is, *sancitus* or *firmatus*, *strengthened, rendered inviolable;* we call saint or holy what is so strongly applied to God, to His worship, to His service that separation is not possible, nor is it permissible to apply it to any other use.

A saint, then, is he whose soul, with all its acts, is so applied to God that there is no separation possible, because the strong bond of the law of charity is there to keep that soul in place.

Firmness also is necessary to sanctity for the reason that the soul applies itself to God as the first principle and last end ; and this application no longer permits mutability, as says St. Paul: "Who then shall separate us from the love of Christ? shall tribulation, or distress, or famine, or nakedness, or danger, or persecution, or the sword? . . . . . . For I am sure that neither death, nor life, etc." (1)

(1) I Rom. viii, 35, 38, 39.

It is not only in holy men that this double element of sanctity is found ; but also in holy things applied to the divine worship, as temples, sacred vessels, etc. But how far greater than that of every material object, is the sanctity of man, when he keeps his mind, his heart, and his body free from all stain, and his whole soul with all its acts firmly applied to God.

III.—Baptism gives to the Christian the beginning of sanctity: for it removes the soul's stains by the remission of sins, and applies it firmly to God, by the infusion of sanctifying grace: *Agios, Sanctus.* Afterwards, the other sacraments are at hand to preserve sanctity, to increase it and even to restore it, if unfortunately mortal sin should come to soil the soul and destroy its union with God. Finally, with the help of actual grace and by the exercise of virtue, the faithful soul rises to an ever increasing sanctity, wherein its purity is ever more exempt from stains, and its adhesion to God is closer and more complete.

But to the ordinary means of becoming holy, the religious profession adds very special resources of great efficacy. Thus to obtain the first element of sanctity, the religious has his three vows, which are so apt to separate him from low and earthy things, and to keep him free from all alloy. The second element also comes to him first and principally from these same vows, which attach him closely to God, and then from his holy rules, which in preserving him, in every detail of his actions, from the danger of stain or separation, continually augment and perfect his union with God.

Sanctity, such as we know it in this world, is never anything but a commencement of sanctity, and this as regards the two parts of which it is composed: for on one side the soul dwells in a house of clay, and the Wise Man says: "The corruptible body is a load upon the soul and the earthly habitation presseth down the mind;" (1) and as it necessarily touches the earth, the use of creatures, which it cannot avoid, always brings some stain, according to the saying of the Wise Man: "A just man shall fall seven times." (2)

On the other side, the adhesion of the soul to God is never out of danger of rupture; for though it be true that on God's side the bond is such as to defy all efforts of enemies, on man's side, alas! how fragile is the tie, since in order to break it only an act of the will is required. Thence the necessity for the saint in this world of completely mistrusting himself and of leaning only upon divine strength in all things. Therefore holiness here below ever claims the soul's attention and diligence; there must be a continual work of reparation, renovation and increase, and the saint upon earth can never say: "I have done enough." Such is God's warning to him, through His prophet: "I have set thee to root up and to

(1) Wisdom, ix, 15.   (2) Prov. xxiv.

pull down, and to build and to plant,'' (1) and to none are these divine words more applicable in truth, continuance and extent, than to the religious in his holy state.

Only in Heaven shall sanctity be perfect and complete in its two parts: there there will be entire exemption from stain and an immovable and eternal adhesion of the soul to the infinitely holy God.

ARTICLE III.

OF THE BOND, OBLIGATION AND THE CESSATION OF THE VOW.

Several important points relating to these questions have already been succinctly explained in the "Catechism on the Vows," (2) this is what we have still to add :

I.—A religious may not bind himself by perpetual vows, when the rule embraced by him prescribes only temporary ones; at least the community shall be in nowise engaged towards him by such vows. It is likewise not allowed for him to bind himself for a time fixed by himself when the rule provides that he shall make perpetual vows. Finally, he can vow no other poverty, chastity and obedience than those marked in the Constitutions of the Order in which he is received. However, if in making the vow of chastity he had the intention of vowing *absolute*, perpetual chastity, or if he had done so before, he would then remain bound,

(1) Jeremias, i, 10.　　　　(2) Part 1st, C. 1.

even in case his superiors should free him from the vow to which they had meant to admit him according to their institute: so that for him to be dispensed from his vow he would have to have recourse to the Sovereign Pontiff.

II.—A thing trivial in every respect may not form the object of a vow made under pain of mortal sin: a slight violation of the rules or a little practice of devotion, for example. God would not accept an exaggerated obligation which reason disavows, and the thing itself would not be susceptible of such an engagement.

A religious may certainly bind himself by vow to observe one or several of his rules, and many fervent souls have set us this example; but they have shown us also that a just discretion should be kept, in this that a careful examination should be made to ascertain whether or not this desire comes from God, that the matter and the meaning of the vow should be clearly determined, and that nothing should be done without the wise direction of spiritual guides. (1) A temporary vow of this kind, to be renewed over and over again, would ordinarily be more discreet, and could be made more easily than a perpetual vow.

A vow to avoid every venial sin may not be made, because the thing is morally impossible, and consequently such a vow would be null. But it is allowed to make a vow to avoid such or

(1) We may see on this subject the vow made by a holy religious, Father de la Colombière, of observing all the rules of his institute. (Journal of his great retreat.)

such venial sins, and even every venial sin that is fully deliberate.

III.—A vow may cease to exist in four ways: through impossibility, annulment, dispensation and commutation.

1st. *Impossibility.* Are there any cases in which the vows of religion cease by this cause? No such impossibility, which of itself can destroy the bond of these vows, is ever seen. But it is different as to their execution and exercise. Thus the case of superior force, as that of the expulsion or the dispersing of a community, leaves unabrogated the bond which obliges the individuals, although for the time being the exercise of all its acts is no longer possible for them. Thus, also, in matters of poverty and obedience, impossibility or a great difficulty of recurring to the superior places the religious in the case of presumed permission, and he may, then, in virtue of this permission, do all that appears to him to be urgent, necessary and even fitting.

The vow of entering into religion ceases by impossibility, as soon as one has been judged inadmissible in the institute one had in view, and there is no obligation imposed by it of offering one's self elsewhere.

2nd. *Annulment.* The right of annulling a vow is different from that of dispensing from it; for the former belongs to the right of domination, and the latter to that of jurisdiction. Thus, a father, a husband, a master, may annul certain vows made by a child, a wife, or a servant, to the prejudice of their rights. The power of jurisdiction belongs only to the Church and to those of her ministers upon whom the Church confers it. A woman, were she superior general or abbess, is incapable of jurisdiction and consequently can never give a dispensation from vows, but, as we shall explain, she can, in virtue of her right of domination, annul certain special vows.

Special or private vows, whatever they may be, made before entering religion, are annulled by the profession of the solemn vows, and only suspended by the profession of the simple vows; in the second case, they would again become obligatory, for whosoever should leave the Order or the congregation. (1)

When a religious has made profession of the solemn vows, his superior has the right to annul any special or personal vow he could afterwards make. The perpetual vows of religion, although simple, seem manifestly to confer the same right on the superior, for the reason is the same, namely, that the will of the inferior having become totally dependent on his, the former cannot lessen by a special vow the power that the superior has acquired over all his acts. And this right which belongs to the power of domination, not of jurisdiction, may be exercised by any superior, so that every private vow is necessarily accompanied by this reservation. "Unless my superior, or superioress, objects." And since these vows are

(1) See again the "Catechism on the Vows," Part I, ch. I.

annulled, they will not revive even in case of dismissal or departure.

Finally, what must be said of a special vow made by a religious who has pronounced only temporary vows of religion? The answer seems to be, that if the obedience vowed temporarily is a universal obedience, every special vow may still be annulled by the superior, since the reason alleged above is here equally in force. But if this vow bore on a matter which should still subsist after the expiration of the temporary engagement, it would then only be suspended, and would become obligatory for him who should leave the congregation.

As to the vows of religion, there are institutes in which superiors can annul them, even without possessing the power of jurisdiction, and consequently without that of dispensation : such are the congregations with approved rules attributing to them the right of annulling simple vows by *the very fact of the legitimate dismissal of a subject*. But for this annulment, superiors must carefully remark that the dismissal must be *legitimate*, that is, founded on the motives of exclusion established by the constitutions themselves.

When a religious obliges his superiors by his wicked conduct to dismiss him and to free him from his vows, let him know, that besides the sins of which he may have rendered himself guilty against other obligations of conscience in this affair, he commits a very grievous and special one against the charity that he owes to himself, by causing the loss of his vocation and by thereby exposing his salvation out of the way that had been opened to him by divine goodness. For, if it be true, that in relation to his eternal salvation, this way is not for him a sort of geometrical line, which once left, he may no longer hope for divine help, it must nevertheless, be said, that in leaving the providential plan traced out for him by God, he puts himself out of the current of abundant help which had been prepared for him in that path, and that consequently he greatly exposes himself to fail finally in saving his soul.

3d. *Dispensation.* The head of the Church only has the power to grant a dispensation from the solemn vows of religion. Every bishop, in his own diocese, possesses the ordinary power to dispense from simple vows, excepting the five that are reserved to the Pope, among which it suffices to name the perpetual vow of absolute chastity. The simple vows of religion, even the temporary ones, in institutes approved by the Holy See, must also be excepted.

As to the vow of entering religion it is also reserved to the Pope, but only when it is a vow of entering into a religious order properly so called; and we know by the declaration of the Holy See, that this case no longer exists in our days as applied to any community of women in France. *

4th. *Commutation of Vows.* According to theology every person has the right to com-

* We believe the same applies to the United States.

mute his own vow into one evidently better, by the very fact that the second virtually encloses the first. This is a certain principle, although in its application prudence often requires that one should not trust altogether to one's own judgment. Hence as a general proposition, comes the right possessed by every religious of passing to a more perfect institute: which is nothing but the commutation by himself of his vows into better vows. But this application of the principle requiring further consideration, we shall return to this weighty matter more explicitly further on. (1)

CHAPTER II.

ON THE EXCELLENCE OF THE VOWS OF RELIGION AND THE STATE OF PERFECTION.

ARTICLE I.

EXCELLENCE OF THESE VOWS.

SECTION I.—*The Vows of Religion compared with other Vows.*

We shall not here treat at length of the different kinds of vows. Nevertheless let us indicate the principal distinctions.

We recognize the *personal* vow, and the *real* vow, the *absolute* vow, and the *conditional* vow, the *perpetual* vow, and the *temporary* vow, the *common* vow, and the *special* vow of religion.

(1) Chapter III, art. IV.

The personal vow imposes its obligation exclusively to the person making it, and this obligation is not transmissible to any other.

The real vow makes the obligation fall directly on the object that is promised to God, so that the obligation may be transmitted to another person and become obligatory on him; for example, an heir.

The vow is absolute when something is promised to God without any condition, it is conditional if the execution of the thing promised depends on some condition. It is only in case the condition is fulfilled, that the conditional vow is obligatory.

The vow is perpetual when one means to bind oneself for life. It is temporary when the engagement is only for a time.

The common vow is one in which any good work is promised to God.

The vow of religion is the one by which the promise of entering into religion is made to God, and the vows of religion are those by which poverty, chastity, and obedience are promised to God in that same state.

The vows of religion contain the most perfect, the most agreeable homage to God, and consequently the most meritorious, after martyrdom, that man can offer in this world to the Divine Majesty. They are as a bouquet of the most sweet fragrance to the Lord, and none can equal its beauty in His sight. This bouquet is composed of three necessary and inseparable flowers, and it can be made only in the religious state, wherein are found, moreover, abundant means of preserving it from all harm, of keeping up its freshness, of daily increasing its brilliancy, and of still setting it off by all the accessory ornaments of which it is susceptible.

That the three vows of religion are an engagement to all that is most elevated in the doctrine of Jesus Christ or Christian morals, that is, an engagement to the practice of the *evangelical counsels*, is the manifest proof of this eulogium. But here, several explanations are necessary.

SECTION II.—*The Evangelical Counsels.*

I.—What is generally meant by the evangelical counsels?

We must recall in order that this may be better understood, what we have already explained, that there are two kinds of sanctity on earth: the one, reduced to its essential elements, consists in not being detached from God by mortal sin; the other rises to a higher degree of purity and union with Him. Two sorts of means correspond to these two sorts of sanctity: some are rigorously exacted by God, the others are only dependent upon His will and good pleasure. Therefore besides our obligatory actions, there is a crowd of others by which we may please the Lord, that are not prescribed by any law. And even in the acts commanded, more or less perfection, purity and care may be added to what is of rigorous obligation both by the intention brought to bear upon them

and by the manner of doing them. Jesus
Christ in His gospel and the Holy Ghost by the
good movements He suggests interiorly to our
hearts, invite us to this; and these invitations
are what are termed *counsels* in opposition to
what is comprised under the name of *precepts*.

II.—There are two distinct kinds of evangelical counsels: some having only special matters
or particular acts as their object; the others
embracing a general, or, so to say, universal
matter.

Thus Jesus Christ gives special counsels
when He tells us to bless those who curse us,
to do good to our enemies, even in the case
wherein we are not so bound by the precept,
to turn the left cheek to those who have struck
us on the right, etc. There are in every virtue
and even in every commandment of God, special
counsels inviting us to do what is beyond the
duty of conscience, either as regards such or
such a circumstance, or as regards what relates
to a more or less perfect intention, the more or
less multiplied number of acts, the greater or
lesser fervor with which we may act. Finally,
it is also a special counsel to engage oneself by
vow to any good work, whether free, or commanded: if free, you impose upon yourself a
duty not imposed by God; if commanded, you
add to the already existing obligation a new
one of your own choice; and thus in order to
be more pleasing to the Lord, you multiply the
ties that bind you to Him.

The counsels that embrace a general and, as it were, universal matter are precisely the three that are given to us in the Gospel by Jesus Christ, regarding poverty, chastity, obedience, and the accomplishment of which extends over one's whole life so as to make it a special kind of life.

Suarez (1) remarks, that ordinarily the special counsels have the same object as the precepts. It is only by reason of circumstances that they become simply counsels: to love our enemies, for example, and to do good to those who persecute us, is a commandment on certain occasions, and only a counsel on others; whilst the three counsels now spoken of are altogether outside the precepts. The first, as St. Thomas again explains, (2) belong to perfection already acquired and their observance proceeds from the superabundance of charity. The second, on the contrary, are general means serving to the acquisition of perfection by furnishing proper instruments to all the virtues especially to charity. Hence is it that Our Lord Jesus Christ chose those last three to oppose them to the three concupiscences, which are the three great obstacles to perfection. Hence also the reason why they are properly and especially called the evangelical counsels, and it is the practice of this sublime portion of the Gospel, which causes those engaging themselves thereto by state of life in the Church to be

(1) De Religione, lib. I, c. 8.
(2) 2a, 2æ, q. 186, a. 2.

called "the chosen portion of the flock of Jesus Christ."

III.—Cannot a person, without being a religious, vow to God poverty, chastity, and obedience?

1st. It is easy to see that out of the religious state, the keeping of the three evangelical counsels can only be partial, that it must necessarily remain incomplete, and that it will never have that character of universality that embraces the entire life with all its acts. He who lives in the world is not in a position to practice poverty and obedience and therefore not in a position to make a vow of them in an absolute manner; and, considering the necessities of life, the exercise made of them by him can only be a special practice of the evangelical counsels. That they may have their whole perfection and the fullness of their execution, what Our Lord Himself said must be done: If you would be perfect, (1) go, that is leave the world; sell all that you have, that is strip yourself of all ownership, and come into a place and state, in which, possessing nothing, without ever ceasing to be totally poor, you shall nevertheless always find the necessaries of life, thanks to the attentions of my Providence; and there you shall equally find it easier to follow me in the perfection of chastity: but you shall, above all, find the means of becoming like me obedient even unto death, and

(1) If thou wilt be perfect, go, sell what thou hast and give to the poor . . . and come follow me. Matt. xix, 21.

by the most universal subjection of your will of consecrating to Me your entire life.

2nd. Without being a religious, it is possible to devote oneself, in a certain measure more or less wide, to the practice of the three evangelical counsels, and God sometimes invites some souls to this without calling them to the religious life on that account. But then much light and watchfulness are required to discern precisely what is His holy will, and much discretion is needed in order to fix the just limits to be imposed upon oneself: so that a director, wise according to God, is almost always indispensable in things so delicate.

Thus, God has raised up in His Church admirable examples of evangelical poverty, even out of the religious state, either consecrated by a special vow, or having an ardent charity as its sole bond. Who does not know St. Alexis and the Blessed Benedict-Joseph Labre, whose heroic mendicity has just been glorified by the Holy See?

Chastity can be vowed out of the religious state, as is proved by the constant practice of the Church; and many secular persons may be called to this life by God. Nevertheless it is only with great circumspection, and after having well considered all the circumstances as to the present and the future, that this perpetual vow should be made in the world. In this matter a temporary vow is of a nature to be more easily allowed, and even there seems to be no reason why this consolation, merit or help should be refused to a good soul thereunto apparently inclined by grace. All objection will disappear if only a short space is embraced at a time, after which it can always be seen whether or not it be suitable to renew the engagement.

Finally, Suarez tells us (1) that without being a religious it is possible to vow obedience to another, for example, to a confessor : either on condition of its being accepted by the other, or even without this acceptance being a necessary condition. It would be most suitable, however, that the one to whom this obedience is vowed should be informed of it in order that he may be more circumspect in his commands. However, no one can be made to change his actual state, in virtue of this vow, as to marry, to become a religious, or not to enter into religion ; in a word, obedience for him, must remain within the limits of his condition, and nothing can be prescribed to him out of accordance with his ordinary duties. Even a Prelate or a religious may, within the same limits, vow to God this kind of obedience to another man, as was done by St. Teresa in regard to her confessors.

SECTION III.—*The Religious Profession compared to Baptism.*

"The Religious profession is a second baptism;" thus speak the holy Doctors; and the reason given by them is that it produces three

(1) De Relig., lib. X, c. 3.

similar effects: it effaces sin, it causes the old man to die, and it communicates a new life.

I.—The religious profession, just as baptism does, remits all sin; this is the common doctrine of theologians, following St. Thomas and St. Antonius. So full and entire a condonation is then made of all temporal punishment due to sin, that were a religious to die immediately after his profession, he would go straight to Heaven, without having any Purgatory to fear. And the Angel of the schools remarks (1) that this remission of sins is not gratuitous as in baptism; but that it is the fruit of the greatest satisfaction that man can offer to God, since at that moment he sacrifices all to Him, in sacrificing himself. (2)

St. Anselm relates the fact of a religious who appeared to his brethren and related to them the struggle he had had to sustain with the devil at the moment of death. He seemed already to be before the tribunal of God and the enemy of salvation had presented himself to accuse him; but some one from Heaven also appeared to defend him. Satan having brought up against him the faults he had committed before baptism, (he had received it when an adult), the accused replied that the holy water had effaced them: which was confirmed by the

(1) In 4, sent. Dist. 4, q. 3, a. 3.

(2) It seems just that a fervent renovation of vows should share proportionately in the merit of their first profession, and that every one may hope for this participation according to the measure of the dispositions which he brings to the renewal.

heavenly defender. The enemy fell back upon other sins committed after baptism; but the religious thought to silence him, by repeating what had been told to him, that nothing of them remained since the day of his profession, and in fact his defender sustained him by a demonstration without reply. Finally, the devil having wished to make the faults committed in the course of his religious life count against him, the dying man again had his ready answer, supported as before by his celestial advocate, which was that they had been covered by means of his careful confessions and by the very works of the religious life.

A very similar fact is related by St. Athanasius in the life of St. Anthony.

II.—The religious profession just as baptism does, gives death to the old man. In fact: 1st. the religious then dies to the world and to all that is of the world. The threefold renouncement of Satan, his pomps and his works, is even much more energetic and much more complete in the profession of the vows than in the baptismal promises, and the triple concupiscence which is the life of the old man receives there a much more vigorous stroke.

2nd. The religious, by the engagement of his vows, ceases to be what he was towards men, so much so that formerly the law declared him dead as regards his rights as a citizen. From that day he is no longer of the world, and the world no longer knows him; and if he wished to reappear therein, he would be looked upon and be treated as a stranger, out of his place, as one dead who had returned among the living.

3rd. But, above all, God no longer keeps account of the past in regard to a man who has devoted himself to Him in such a way. In His sight, the religious, no less than the newly baptized, is buried in the tomb with Jesus Christ, and in that state wherein he sees him, as His Beloved Son, disengaged from his old effects, He finds nothing in him of what formerly wounded His Divine Eyes, notwithstanding the remains of concupiscence still felt by him and left him for combat and merit. (1)

III.—The profession of the vows, as the Apostle again says of holy baptism, (2) causes the religious to pass to a new life. After having too often, by his worldly life, been like the first Adam and earthly like him, the religious on the day of his vows begins to resemble the second Adam, and after His example, he sees himself, he feels himself, as if transformed by His grace into a celestial man. (3) Then does

(1) In renatis nihil odit Deus; quia nihil damnationis est iis qui vere consepulti sunt cum Christo per baptisma in mortem. . . . Manere autem concupiscentiam vel fomitem hæc sancta Synodus fatetur et sentit, quæ cum ad agonem relicta sit, nocere non consentientibus, sed viriliter per Christi Jesu gratiam repugnantibus non valet; quinimo qui legitime certaverit coronabitur. Conc. Trid. sess. V, De Pecc., orig. 5.

(2) As Christ is risen from the dead by the glory of the Father, so we also may walk in newness of life. Romans, vi, 4.

(3) The first man was of the earth, earthly; the second man from heaven, heavenly; such as is the earthly, such

all become new to him: new thoughts, new sentiments, new appreciations and new tendencies, new tastes and new enjoyments, new works and a new manner of performing them: so that to him must also be applied what the Council of Trent says of the newly baptized, "He no longer walks according to the flesh, but despoiled of the old man, in all the details of his new life he has, by his profession become innocent, immaculate, pure, without stain and cherished of God." (1)

A passage of St. Bernard will sum up all these considerations: "You wish to learn from me how it is that among all the other means of doing penance, the religious profession has merited the prerogative of being called a second baptism? It is because it is a perfect renunciation of the world, and because the singular excellence of the spiritual life led therein, raises it above all other manner of life on earth: so that religious leaving the likeness of men, assume that of the Angels, and even re-establish in themselves the image of God, by conforming themselves to Jesus Christ, as happens in baptism. But just as this sacrament grasps us away from the power of darkness to transfer us to the Kingdom of eternal light, so by this second regeneration that is produced by so holy an engagement, we escape from the darkness not only

also are the earthly; and such as is the heavenly, such also are they that are heavenly. I Cor. xv, 47, 48.

(1) Qui non secundum carnem ambulant, sed veterem hominem exuentes, innocentes, immaculati, puri, innoxii ac Deo dilecti effecti sunt. Conc. Trid., ibid.

of original sin, but also of many actual sins,
to enter into the light of the virtues, applying
to ourselves anew these words of the Apostle:
'the night has passed and the day has approached.'" (1)

SECTION IV.—*Religious Profession compared to
Martyrdom.*

Speaking of religious devotedness in St.
Paula's epitaph, St. Jerome expresses himself
thus: "It is not only by the effusion of blood that
martyrdom is to be reckoned, but the perfect
service of a soul devoting its life to the Lord is
also a daily martyrdom; the first weaves its
crown with roses and violets, the second forms
its of lilies." (2) If in fact, the martyrdom of
blood is the greatest act of charity that man is
capable of producing, with the aid of grace,

(2) Audire vultis a me unde, inter cætera pœnitentiæ
instituta, monasterialis disciplina meruerit hanc præroga-
tivam, ut secundum baptisma nuncupetur? Arbitror, ob
perfectam mundi abrenuntiationem, et singularem excel-
lentiam vitæ spiritualis, qua præeminens universis vitæ
humanæ generibus hujusmodi conversatio professores suos
angelis similes facit; immo divinam in homine reformat
imàginem, configurans nos Christo instar baptismi. Sed
et quomodo in baptismo eruimur de potestate tenebrarum
et transferimur in regnum claritatis æternæ; ita et in sanc-
tissimi hujus secunda quadam regeneratione propositi, de
tenebris æque non unius originalis sed multorum actuali-
um delictorum, in lumen virtutum evadimus, redaptantes
nobis-illud Apostoli: Nox præcessit, dies autem appropin-
quavit. S. Bernard, Præcepto et Disciplina.

(1) Non solum effusio sanguinis martyrium reputatur,
sed devotæ quoque mentis servitus immaculata quotidia-
num martyrium est: illa corona de rosis et violis texitur,
ista de liliis.

the religious sacrifice, by its daily devotedness, so multiplies acts of charity, that they are capable of equalling and sometimes of surpassing the merit of the shedding of blood.

The martyrdom of blood lasts but a short time, and one great effort may be sufficient to insure its reward; that of the religious profession is generally much longer, and redeems by its duration what is wanting in violence and intensity. It is necessary in it to die daily, according to St. Paul's expression, (1) that is, that therein we must ceaselessly strike redoubled blows at corrupt nature, by *mortification*, which, according to the force of the word, is to operate death. (2)

Martyr signifies *witness:* and what testimony can be more beautiful than that rendered by religious profession, and how glorious it is to God and salutary to men! Glorious to God whose rights to all our services it each instant proclaims; salutary to men, either to our brethren themselves by the daily encouragement of good example, or to the persons of the world, who find therein an eloquent preaching of Christian truth. And in fact, how many times, has not this aspect of virtue recognized and appreciated by the impious, caused faith to re-enter into his soul, and elicited from his will holy resolutions!

(1) I die daily. I Cor. xv, 31.
(2) For thy sake we are put to death all the day long. Romans, viii, 36.

II.—But the religious profession is not a single martyrdom, it contains several at one and the same time.

1st. There is the martyrdom of voluntary poverty. Let us listen to St. Bernard: "Why is it that in the Sermon on the Mount, the same promise is made to the poor and to the martyrs, if not because voluntary poverty is a species of martyrdom?" (1) And with as much truth as energy, he thus describes this martyrdom of religious poverty. Temporal goods were held, with the assurance of the advantages by them procured, and despoliation has given the constraint of poverty and incertitude of the future. Something might, at least, have been acquired, but the very right of receiving what the world might offer, has been taken away. In vain does Satan strive to tempt to cupidity; all hopes have been renounced and his temptations are scorned. But there are, above all, in the human heart that strong and subtle love of ease, that propensity to create imaginary necessities, that desire for the little comforts of life, which are as a continual itching. But self is constantly overcome, every day resistance is made for the love of the Lord to all those prickings of nature. How many crowns! What rights to the riches and delights of Paradise! (2)

(1) Quid sibi vult quod eadem promissio facta est pauperibus et martyribus, nisi quia vere martyrii genus est paupertas voluntaria?

(2) Paupertate premi inter divitias quas affert mundus, quas ostentat diabolus, quas desiderat noster iste appetitus:

2ndly. Religious chastity is even a more glorious and more meritorious martyrdom than poverty. For, says the Holy Spirit, man's life is a warfare on earth; but what is the principal object of this incessant struggle, if not sensuality? Intestine and domestic war in which the enemy is within, always in arms, and never discouraged; wherein even after having fled from exterior occasions and seductions, the flesh still is there tormenting the spirit. What noble testimony, then, does not the perfectly chaste soul render to God, when it thus preserves its treasure in a fragile vessel? Alas, says St. Isidore, "by the vice of impurity, more than by any other, does the devil subjugate mankind;" and St. Augustine observes, "that among all the combats sustained by Christians, the hardest are those of chastity, wherein the struggle is daily and the victory is rare." (1) And yet how many pure souls in religious houses! What vigilance in repulsing the least attack! What fidelity in keeping oneself from the slightest stain! In a word, what glory is rendered to that divine grace that triumphs in infirmity!

3rdly. The third martyrdom of the religious life, obedience, is the most meritorious of all, since it immolates what is best and dearest to

an non merito coronabitur qui sic certaverit, mundum abjiciens promittentem, irridens inimicum tentantem, et quod gloriosius est, de seipso triumphans, et crucifigens concupiscentiam prurientem? Bern., Serm. 1, omnium sanct.

(1) Inter omnia christianorum certamina, duriora sunt prælia castitatis ubi quotidiana est pugna et rara victoria.

man, his own will; it is the most extended and the most continual, since it embraces every action and the whole existence of the religious.

III. — A last and striking consideration on the martyrdom of the religious life to be still presented, is its resemblance to *the crucifixion.* Like Jesus Christ religious are *crucified men;* and it is by the vows that this martyrdom is executed. After having been, so to speak, measured to their future cross during their novitiate, the moment of extending them thereon arrives: it is that of their profession, and they are attached thereunto by three nails; so that they can say with the Apostle: "Our old man is crucified" (1) with the nails of the three vows. And this is how the effects of this spiritual crucifixion are explained by pious authors:

First, a nail, when driven in, begins by pushing out the obstacle met with. The same is done in the soul of the religious by the nails of the holy vows; they drive out unruly affections in a way to destroy in him at the start the body of sin, of which St. Paul speaks. (2)

Then by a second effect, the nails pierce and tear the crucified members; to such an extent, that in consequence of this violent suspension of the whole body on three painful points, life becomes but one continual and universal suf-

(1) Vetus homo noster crucifixus est. Rom. vi, 6.
(2) Our old man is crucified with him, that the body of sin may be destroyed, to the end that we may serve sin no longer. Rom. vi, 6.

fering. And this, in some manner, takes place in the religious life, the three vows being ever there to make themselves felt. It is a state of life and death like that of those on the cross, and the religious, as well as the crucified is, according to the Apostle's saying, a man living and dying at the same time. (1)

The third effect of nails for the sufferer is to hold him so strongly to the cross, that no means are left him of detaching himself, especially if the point has been bent. Is not this done by the vows of religion, principally by the perpetual vows, by the solemn vows, in which all the points are, so to say, bent back! Then and thenceforth the cross can no longer be left, unless one is willing to suffer the terrible laceration of apostasy. Moreover the crucified, so tightly held to his cross, has no longer any liberty in his acts, nor even in his least movement; it is thus with the religious fixed by his holy vows. Finally, when a man is raised on a cross, he is suspended between heaven and earth; and such, from the day of his profession is the situation of the religious in this world: his feet and his senses are still near to the earth, but his head and his mind are close to Heaven; by trial and labor yet of this world, by desire and the certitude of his hope he already lives in the next.

It is related in St. Bernard's life that he one day met a malefactor, laden with chains, who was being taken to the gallows by the soldiers

(1) As dying and behold we live. II Cor. vi, 9.

of the Count of Champagne. The holy Abbot,
moved by an inspiration from on high, approaches the archers and begged them to turn
over this man unto him, assuring them that he
would chastise him as he deserved. The re-
quest provoked astonishment, and whilst he
was insisting to overcome the soldiers' refusal,
the Count of Champagne, who was hunting in
the neighboring forest, coming up unexpectedly, after having saluted the Saint with ven-
eration was very much surprised at the repeti-
tion of his proposition. "What! holy father,"
exclaimed the prince, "you must not know
what a rascal it is in whom you have taken an
interest!" Forthwith he related the transgres-
sions of the man, for which, he added, he
assuredly deserves hanging. "I admit all
that," smilingly replied the Saint, "and that is
just why I propose to inflict upon him his chastisement myself, that will be not one but many
deaths." At last, he succeeded in having the
culprit turned over to him and led him to
Clairvaux. A victorious grace had already
penetrated the heart of this man, the holy
Abbot's charity was so blessed, that the malefactor, after an exemplary conversion, was
judged worthy of being admitted among the
religious; and there, during more than thirty
years, he verified St. Bernard's words, inflict-
ing upon himself with his own hands, by rigorous austerities the chastisement which other
hands would have caused him to endure but
once.

ARTICLE II.

ON THE RELIGIOUS STATE OR STATE OF PERFECTION.

SECTION I.—*In what a State precisely consists, and especially the Religious State.*

I.—The word *state, status,* comes from the Latin Verb *stare, to stand;* and the name *state* is therefore proper for a certain position taken by a thing having regard for the requirements of its nature so that it may be suitably in a sort of fixity and repose. Thus a man is said to stand *stat,* when having his feet resting securely below and his head raised above, all the members of his body are in a suitable disposition of steady equilibrium and immobility. (1)

In the moral order, things extrinsic to man and easily variable, do not constitute in his regard what may be called a state; but a state must affect his very person, when on account of a fixed or permanent cause, he becomes master of himself or dependent on others. This is why a state is said to suppose a certain condition of servitude or liberty.

An office, a charge, a dignity are not states, because they can be taken or left, and do not affect the very condition of a person.

An office is properly so-called on account of *the acts* therein exercised : for example, the one filling the office of judge is appointed to pronounce sentences. But a state means a posi-

(1) 2a, 2æ, q. 183, a. 1.

tion inherent in the person according as it makes him free or dependent. If certain charges, certain employments are called states, it is only on account of the subjection and fixity or permanency therein involved.

Thus there is the state of grace and the state of sin. In the first, St. Paul tells us that man is liberated from sin and subject to justice; in the second he shakes off the yoke of divine law, to become the slave of sin. (1)

There is the state called by theology the state of *traveller*, and the state of *comprehend* or, one detains man in the condition of the present life's pilgrimage; the other delivers him and places him in the blessed subjection of the beatific vision.

There is the state of marriage that places some under the conjugal law, and the state of continence that hold others back by a contrary engagement.

II.—To come to our subject, there are the *secular state* and the *religious state*. These two states considered relatively to evangelical perfection are called: the first *the common state* or *state of precept*, the second *perfect state* or *state of counsel*.

A secular without being in that latter state, not having subjected himself to it, may nevertheless acquire the interior perfection of it and even in a higher degree than such or such a religious; but the religous has this characteristic that he is bound in a firm and lasting

(1) Romans, vi, 16.

manner to the obligations of his state, that he makes public profession of being in this state, and that he possesses therein most efficacious means of perfection that cannot be had by a person in the world.

The religious state therefore, affects the person, insomuch that by the vows of religion it makes one enter into a position of life that does not change, and this position is at one and the same time a holy servitude and a holy liberty. It is a holy servitude by the happy necessity in which one has voluntarily placed oneself in regard to God and virtue; but the results are in nowise those supposed by worldly minds, namely, the loss or the diminution of true liberty; rather, it is quite the contrary, proofs of which may be read in Rodriguez, (1) therefore is this necessity full of merit for religious? On the other hand it is a holy freedom from the yoke that weighs on so many others; liberation from the world, its seductions, its wants, its vanities; in a certain measure even freedom from concupiscence and sin.

SECTION II.—*The Peculiar Merit of the Religious State.*

I.—In the devotedness to God that is contained in that state, does the merit of a religious life appear. For the very fact of having placed oneself in God's service in an immutable position, and of having voluntarily

(1) On Perfect., part III, 2d treatise, 5 ch.

chained oneself to Him by a holy necessity, makes it manifest that much more is done for the Divine Master, and consequently for oneself than could have been done in the world with even an equal desire of serving God and of sanctifying self.

In fact, God thus receives, according to the language of the Saints, not only the fruits of the tree and of the ground, but the tree and the ground themselves; and who does not know that assuring to some one the ownership of the soil is, without comparison, much more than offering to him its fruits?

Likewise, had this tree remained in the arid earth of the world, it might, like so many others, have been fated to bear little or no fruit; but transplanted near the running waters, (1) all favorable conditions are enjoyed by it for becoming abundantly laden. The soil of the soul, left under an unwholesome influence, or given up to whims, to instability, to sloth, would have been exposed to be overgrown with briars and thistles, whilst specially confided to the Divine Husbandman and placed under the action of His most abundant graces, it gives just hopes of a rich harvest.

Finally, the special merit of religious devotedness consists in its being the highest expression of devotion: for, as we have seen, devotion is nothing but a certain will to give oneself promptly and unreservedly to every thing that belongs to the service of God; and

(1) Psalm i, 3.

nowhere does this promptitude and this plenitude of will appear so much as in the religious
profession. If, for instance, a Christian in the
world has a determination equal to that of
the religious of refusing nothing to the Lord ;
will this purpose be lasting, thus left to itself? Can it, in case of need, be sustained,
excited, revived, as it is in the bosom of a
religious community among brethren who support us when we faint? But even should we
grant it to be as good, as constant, and as pro-
ductive of equal acts of virtue; still must the
merit be less because there is lacking that of
the religious sacrifice.

II.—A curious objection raised by some men
of the world against religious persons must now
be examined. In leaving the world, say they,
you have fled from difficulties, you have shown
a want of courage and your virtue being more
easy will therefore be less meritorious.

We ought first to ask the speakers, if it is really in order to merit more that they restrain
themselves from abandoning the world.

We might add, that if they and others can
triumph over the world whilst remaining in
the midst of its dangers, others more diffident,
feel above all the necessity they are in of fleeing
from those same dangers, and make their first
merit consist in making sure of their eternal
interests.

But St. Thomas gives us a more instructive
and complete reply. (1)

(1) 2a, 2æ, q. 184, a. 8, ad 6m.

We must distinguish two sorts of difficulties in regard to virtue: one belonging to the work itself, when it is arduous; the other proceeding from exterior obstacles.

The first effectively increases the merit, because this proceeds from the very excellence of the work which is to be done.

As to the second kind of difficulty that proceeds from without, it sometimes diminishes the perfection of virtue, other times it is the indication of more perfect virtue. In those not loving virtue enough to be willing to disengage themselves from the things that produce the obstacles, it diminishes the perfection of virtue. In him who seeing himself unexpectedly or forcibly in presence of an obstacle, remains faithful to virtue, it is a sign of a more perfect virtue.

It is manifest that the first kind of difficulty which increases merit, exists much more in the religious state than in any other, since all that is most arduous and most perfect in the Christian life is therein aimed at. As for the difficulty of the second kind, it is most true that religious strive in every way to escape from it in every case and this is an effect of their wisdom, as well as a proof of their love of virtue, and the special matter of their merit. Besides they do not deny that those who are compelled to remain in presence of difficulties can give signs of a still greater virtue, if really faithful.

III.—In support of this answer, let us add still a great principle of the same St. Thomas,

which is everywhere of frequent application
in the service of God. Virtue, he tells us,
consists less in the difficulty encountered than
in the good done: so that the greatness of a
virtuous act is rather to be measured by its
goodness than by its difficulty, for it is *the good
act*, rather than *the difficult act*, which counts
for merit; whence it follows that we must consider as most meritorious, not what is more
difficult or more painful, but that which is at
the same time more difficult and better, or
which draws from its difficulty an increase of
goodness. (1)   Now, goodness flows from three
things; from the goodness of the object, from
the goodness of the intention, and from charity.   The martyrs, for example, merited much
in suffering for Jesus Christ; but the Blessed
Virgin merited more than all of them by her
least acts, although perhaps there was not always suffering in them.   And this is a practical truth that offers a real direction for the
consolation of those souls to whom it is not
given to suffer as much for God as they would
desire.

IV.—Another teaching of the angelic Doctor
will complete the question of the merit of the
religious state; he addresses himself to those

(1) Ibid., q. 123, a. 12; et q. 27, a. 8.   Ratio virtutis magis
consistit in bono quam in difficili; unde magis mensuranda
est virtutis magnitudo secundum rationem boni quam dif-
ficilis.—Plus facit ad rationem meriti bonum quam diffi-
cile; unde non oportet quod omne quod est difficilius, sit
magis meritorium; sed quod sic est difficilius, ut sit etiam
melius.

who are more preoccupied by the sight of their past sins and the need they feel of doing penance for them, than by the thought or the desire of perfection. These are his words: "The religious state has, without doubt, been instituted principally for the acquisition of perfection, and this is why exercises and means removing obstacles to perfect charity are found therein.

But by the very fact that these obstacles are removed, so with greater reason are the causes of sin which totally destroys charity also removed. And as in this does penance properly and principally consist, namely in diminishing the causes of sin, it follows that no state is more proper to penance than the religious state. Thus Canon law cites the example of a great culprit who was advised rather to enter a monastery than to undergo public penance whilst remaining in the world; and the reason given is that penance there is as a whole, both better and slighter." (1)

We shall not repeat what has been said above as to the satisfactory works which the religious profession gives us occasion of performing for the expiation of sin.

SECTION III.—*On an essential condition for the merit of the religious in his state.*

Although the great act of profession of vows be of excellent merit before God, nevertheless a truth which cannot be too often repeated to those who have made this act is, that its merit,

(1) 2a, 2æ, q. 185, a. 8.   (2) Ch. II, art. II, sect. III.

not to become illusory, exacts an indispensable condition, namely, that of the accomplishment and of fidelity in keeping this promise. As it is not the habit that makes the religious, so it is not the perfection of his state that gives him his personal perfection, but the performance of the duties of his state. Let us again allow St. Thomas to speak. (1) Some persons, he tells us, without being in the state of perfection, can be perfect, and others may be in the state of perfection yet be far from perfect. The state of perfection is one thing, and perfection of life another. A person is said to be in the state of perfection, not because he effectually possesses perfect charity, but because he is bound to deeds of perfection. It happens that some persons impose obligations upon themselves that they do not keep, whilst others do the good to which they are not obliged; as is told us in the Gospel of the two sons whom their father sent to work in his vineyard, one answered: "I will not," and later he went nevertheless; whilst the other having answered: "I go, sir," notwithstanding did not go. (2)

We must ever return to these two words of the Psalm: *vovete et reddite*. (3) "Yes," says the Lord to those whom He calls, "offer me your vows of religion, no other offering can be more pleasing to Me, but on the condition of being faithfully accomplished. Nothing is so easy, nothing so quickly done as to pronounce

(1) 2a, 2æ, q. 184, a. 4.
(2) Matthew, xxi, 28, 29, 30, 31.   (3) Psalm lv.

the words of the formula, *Voveo*, etc.; but to be
true to them, that is the great point, (1) and it
takes in one's whole life. If unfortunately you
should afterwards forget what you have promised; if you should neglect the obligations of
your holy vows, not only would you, yourself,
destroy all the merit of your profession, but
you would also make it the matter of a judgment still more rigorous; for says the wise
man: "An unfaithful and foolish promise dis-
pleases God; and it is much better not to vow,
than after a vow not to perform the things
promised." (2)

Old religious are sometimes heard to speak
with a certain complacency of the number of
their years of profession; this vanity is more
than ridiculous, if their manner of living in religion agrees little with their age.

SECTION IV.—*For an institute to belong to the Religious State it must have the approbation of the
Church.*

I.—Why every institute and pious corpora-
tion needs to be approved by the Church in
order to belong to the religious state, is easily
understood. In fact, let us suppose that a number of the faithful gather together with the
thought of tending conjointly toward evangelical perfection. But they need the assurance
that the true way will be shown them; they
need a warranty on the legitimacy of the means

(1) Hoc opus, hic labor est. Virg.
(2) Ecclesiastes, v, 3, 4.

proposed to attain the end. This assurance, this warrant can be given by no man whatsoever, were he animated with the best intentions, even were he a Saint. Hence the necessity of recourse to the Church, of its approbation; for it is infallible as well when it pronounces on a law of manners, as when it establishes a doctrine of faith.

Moreover, this gathering of men wish to constitute a religious body with its special form, with the right of self-government and of increasing according to its constitutions; for all which things the intervention and authority of the Church are again necessary.

This is why, as Suarez teaches, the approbation of an institute by the Church contains two things; the first a *doctrinal judgment* by which it at least implicitly declares that the end of the new foundation is holy, its means for obtaining this end wise and good; in a word, that the kind of life traced out by it is fitted to conduct souls to the special perfection it has in view. The second thing contained in this approbation is *an act of jurisdiction* by which the Church according to this judgment constitutes it into a religious body, providing it with all things necessary to its existence, its government and the development of its life.

Since the General Councils of Lateran and Lyons, the approbation of the Holy See is necessary, at least for every religious order properly so-called. In approving it, the Pope, by the very fact, becomes in an exclusive manner its first superior and prelate; it is he who communicates to Superiors the power they are to exercise, and who accepts through them the vows of all those therein admitted.

II.—Simple religious congregations, for similar reasons, need to be approved likewise by the Church, and this approbation must come from at least episcopal authority. When a congregation is approved by a bishop in his diocese, he becomes its first superior, from whom all powers proceed; but if this congregation were to spread into other dioceses, it must depend similarly upon the respective Ordinaries of the places for those of its houses that are there located.

When a congregation solicits the approbation of the Holy See, the following order is generally kept by the Sovereign Pontiff: he first grants *the decree of eulogium*, which is as the germ of the formal approbation to be expected; he, later on, approves the fundamental points of the institute and constitutes it by apostolic authority, or he even then examines and approves the body of the constitutions.

The approbation of the Holy See does not change a simple congregation into a religious body, properly so-called, unless such should be the expressed will and declaration of the head of the Church. The effects of this approbation are: 1st, to give more authority to the rule and more stability to its existence; 2d, to authorize it to make foundations in every part of the Church, with the consent of the

Ordinaries; 3d, to prevent any change or modification being made, by inferior authority, in its approved constitutions, its end and its means of arriving thereat; 4th, to oblige it to have recourse to the Holy See in any extraordinary occurrence or important act of its government.

Thus, as has been recently declared by the Holy See, on several occasions in regard to congregations of women, the dispensation of vows, even though they be simple or temporary, is reserved to it. Its authorization is necessary for the alienation of the real estate of the congregation, for the transferring elsewhere of the Institute's mother-house, for the foundation of a new novitate, for the division of the congregation into provinces, and for the deposition of a superior-general. Finally, every three years an account of *the material and personal state* indicating the number of houses and of religious; of *the disciplinary state,* touching the observance of the constitutions and the training of Novices; and of *the economic state,* touching the administration of temporal goods, is to be sent to Rome.

The episcopal authority over religious institutes approved by the Holy See, is defined by the Council of Trent and by the decrees of Sovereign Pontiffs. We shall speak more especially of communities of women.

For the establishment of a religious house in a diocese, the permission of the Ordinary is necessary: But the Holy See does not generally approve of a bishop being superior-general, or of naming some one to exercise this function over a pious institute extending out of his diocese, in order not to infringe the rights of other bishops.

The bishop of a place prescribes or approves everything touching the ecclesiastical functions in chapels of the institute, and appoints the chaplains who are to preside thereat. He assigns the confessors of the community, ordinary and extraordinary. And no Sister, except when travelling, may apply for absolution to any priest but those by him approved for nuns. (1)

He makes, either himself or by a delegate, the canonical examination of the novices, such as is prescribed by the Council of Trent: that is " he examines carefully the will of each, or causes it to be thus examined, as well before the clothing as before the profession, to assure himself that she is neither constrained nor misled and that she knows what she is doing."

Finally, he is established by the Council of Trent to govern the communities of women in his diocese, as *delegate of the Holy See*. In this quality he visits the houses, either in person or by another, he presides at the general chapters and confirms the election of the superior-general ; and he transmits an account of these assemblies to the Sacred Congregation of Bishops and Regulars.

(1) We use this word in its wider sense.

III.—The approbation given to a religious body by the Church must be the object of a serious consideration for every one of its members, on account of the practical consequences that flow therefrom: for nothing is more capable of exciting confidence in God, nourishing the peace of the soul in its vocation, attaching the religious to his holy state and finally of inspiring him with the spirit of obedience. This should be the first thing brought to the notice of a postulant.

Every religious should always recognize this authority of the Church and respect it everywhere and in all things in his institute; it will be to him a great and precious exercise of the spirit of Faith, since he will see ceaselessly realized those words of Our Lord: "He who hears you, hears Me." But every child of the Church is likewise bound to recognize with respect its authority in every religious institute: for to attack or to despise an order or a rule approved by it is to fail in respect for it and to sin against religion.

Let us also remark the solicitude of the Church for religious institutes. This is in fact, because therein is involved the service of God in all that is highest and most perfect: therein it sees the portion of the flock that is dearest to the Divine Shepherd; therein, finally, the experience of centuries show it the places in which sanctity has flourished with the greatest abundance and splendor. What is not, therefore its zeal in maintaining or reviving regular observance. Let the many councils that have legislated on this subject, the many decrees of Sovereign Pontiffs, and the acts of many pious bishops give testimony ! Since the Church of God, then, loves the religious state and religious institutes with so special an affection, any one having other sentiments, in their regard, is certainly not animated with its spirit, and whoever he may be his example can be of no weight when put in the balance against its. If blemishes and even abuses and defections are met with in a religious body, the Church knows how to make allowance for human weakness before the elevated end to be aimed at, and instead of ceasing to esteem the institute or to love the state, it rather labors to restore discipline and fervor. Thus should its true children feel and think, instead of maliciously taking occasion of the faults of individuals to hate and to depreciate the state and the body.

ARTICLE III.

RELIGIOUS PERFECTION.

SECTION I.— *What is to be exactly understood by perfection.*

Mention is often made of perfection, of the desire for perfection, of the necessity of becoming perfect, yet the idea of perfection is but too often so vague that the imagination gives way to pure illusions, producing only useless sentiments and sterile results.

The following are the fundamental and precise ideas of perfection, according to the Angelic Doctor: A thing is called *perfect* to which nothing is wanting. *Perfectum est id cui nihil deest.*—Three kinds of perfection are to be distinguished. The first consists in the object being so constituted in its own being, that nothing is wanting to it, according to its nature. Thus man has this perfection, when he possesses a soul endowed with all its faculties and a body endowed with all its senses and all its members.—The second perfection gives to the object all that can be added to its substance so that nothing may be wanting to it of the bounty of nature. Thus a man has this perfection when he possesses all the qualities of soul and body that he can naturally have.—The third perfection consists in this that the object attains its proper end in order to find therein every good that its condition can exact. Thus a watch is perfect when it reaches its end, which is to keep time exactly, and a man is perfect when he attains his last end, which is God, the sovereign Good. We shall treat of this third perfection relatively to man, because it is his *moral perfection* towards which he must tend to find happiness; it is nothing else but *the perfection of his virtue* and *the perfection of his beatitude.*

Every being is then perfect when it attains its proper end, because the end of a being, once reached, gives it its final perfection. Now, it is through charity that man reaches

God, his last end, according to these words of
St. John: (1) "He that abideth in charity
abideth in God and God in him." Consequently the perfection of the Christian life is
especially in Charity.

But an object may be termed perfect in two
ways: first, in an absolute manner, considering the perfection of the thing in what belongs to its very substance. Secondly, an object is said to be perfect under such or such
an aspect, when it is the perfection in the
accidents of the object, that is, in all that is
overadded to its substance, that is considered.
It is thus, for example, that when a body is
perfect as to its substance, and perfectly white,
two distinct and very different perfections are
found therein. The first perfection is the substantial and principal perfection of the object,
the second is its accidental or secondary perfection.

Now the Christian life consists substantially
in charity, according to St. John: "He who
loveth not, remaineth in death." (2) Whence
it follows that the perfection of the Christian
life, in its absolute idea, is to be considered
according to charity. It is afterwards to be
considered, in a secondary manner and by way
of complement, as to the other virtues that a
perfect man should possess. (3)

II.—Let us insist on the practical consequences flowing from these principles. First,

(1) I John, iv, 16.   (2) I John, v.
(3) 2a, 2æ, q. 184, a. 1.

religious perfection is according to charity;
let us remember that charity is a virtue by
which we love God above all things, because
He is our sovereign Good and our neighbor as
ourselves for the love of God. Charity has
then one sole motive, God only, and a double
object, God and our neighbor. We must, consequently, be careful, when considering charity
and its perfection, neither to forget either of
these two objects, nor to lose sight of its sole
end, which must be God alone.

You enter religion for the purpose of acquiring there the perfection of the Christian life;
there you bind yourself by your state to tend
towards this perfection, which is principally
perfection as to charity. Be, therefore, mind-
ful of your double obligation, namely, of
ceaselessly aiming not only at the perfection
of the love of God, but also at that of the love
of your neighbor. The exterior and in some
way material practice in reference to each of
these may be different according to the diversity of the institutes and of their special
works; but it is towards what is perfect in
this double relation that religious persons are
bound ever to tend. It is to make clear the
road that they must follow that we are about
to set forth at an adequate length all this
great matter of charity, the perfection of which
is the obligatory term of their efforts.

On the other hand, religious perfection depends also upon the other virtues, secondarily,
it is true, but necessarily also in order that

nothing may be wanting to it. Therefore, in the same way, we ought to enter here upon the consideration of all Christian virtues, but as this subject is so vast and as it would cause us to lose sight of the explanation of the "The Catechism of Vows," we refer our readers to the ascetic writers, by whom it has been fully treated.

SECTION II.—*The Primary Object of Charity or Divine Love.*

§ I. *In what divine love consists.* (1)

1st. In general, love is nothing else than *complacency in good*, or rather to speak more clearly, it is the movement of the heart attaching itself to an object that appears to it to be good. To love a thing, therefore, is to take complacency in that thing, that is to say, it is to attach oneself to it because it is found to be good.

To love some one, is also to wish him well, because in the love of friendship, there is not only attachment to the person of the friend, but moreover and by a necessary consequence, benevolence in his regard as to another self.

There are two clear ideas characterizing divine love, which is a love of friendship: to love God is to attach oneself to Him because one finds Him to be good, and it is to wish Him well.

2ndly. Four different shades may be distinguished in the general idea of divine love: love, dilection, charity and friendship.

(1) 2a, 2æ, quæst. 26, art. 1 and 3.—2a, 2æ, q. 23, a. 1.

Love is properly what we have just defined.

Dilection adds the idea of *election, diligere,* that is *ex diversis eligere, to choose among many:* consequently dilection is found only in the reasonable appetite, wherein is liberty. It also expresses *the act* of the love of charity rather than its *habit.*

St. Denis tells us that with regard to God, the name love is more divine than that of dilection, because it expresses, so to say, something passive: and in fact in divine love, man is rather borne towards God by undergoing His attraction, than capable of going to Him by his reason and by his own choice, therefore is this love obtained principally by prayer.

Charity indicates a certain perfection of love, insomuch as the object loved is esteemed as *dear* or *cherished* and of great price; thence comes the fact, that the name charity is given only to that love that places God above all things.

Friendship expresses the habit of charity and also the mutual attachment binding two hearts to each other with a reciprocal benevolence. Now charity is a friendship that is formed between God and man, according to these words of St. James: "Abraham was called the friend of God;" (1) and Our Lord Jesus Christ declares to His own that they are "His friends." (2)

This mutual alliance between God and man is founded on the communication of His beati-

(1) James, ii, 23.
(2) I have called you friends. John, xv, 15.

tude by God to man, here below by sanctifying grace which is its germ, and in Heaven by glory and the full enjoyment of Himself. And man makes God the return of which he is capable, by communicating and consecrating to God what he has, what he is and all that he can give to Him.

It belongs to friendship to live with one's friend. Thus man enters into a continual relation with God through charity and this is the exercise of his spiritual life on earth. But during the exile these relations of divine friendship are imperfect, because as St. Paul tells us, "we know only in part" (1) and because the Divine Friend remains behind the Veil of Faith. And yet what great things have taken place between God and his saints! How stupendous a familiarity (2) says the author of the *Imitation;* and this is proportionally felt by every fervent and generous soul. In our true home, the relations of divine friendship shall be perfect, "when we shall see His Face," and "He shall be all in all." (3)

§ II.—*The seat of divine love is solely in the will and not in man's lower appetite.* (4)

Two powers tending towards good in order to delight therein and to become attached thereto, exist in the human soul: they are named by philosophers the two *appetites* of

(1) I Cor. xiii, 9.　　(2) Familiaritas stupenda nimis.
(3) Apoc. xxii, 4; I Cor. xv, 28.
(4) 1a, 2æ, q. 26, a. 1.

our nature; one is *the inferior appetite*, the other *the reasonable or superior appetite*, also called *the will*.

These two powers of the soul have each the faculty of loving; but their love is as different as they themselves are; the one loves necessarily, the other voluntarily, both have good for their object, but each in its own way: for the object of the lower appetite is a good of which the senses can lay hold, whilst that of the reasonable appetite is a good held or known by the understanding under the common idea of good.

Now, the object of charity is no sensible good, but the Divine Good, God Himself, Who cannot be known by means of the senses, but only by man's intelligence. Whence it necessarily follows that the *subject* of charity, that is, the seat of the soul wherein it can reside, is not the inferior appetite, that experiences sensible impressions, but only the will.

These are principles of great importance for the spiritual direction of souls, whether it be necessary to reassure them on the subject of the inclinations to sensible pleasure felt by them without any consent, or to enlighten them on the true nature of charity.

But what are then these sweet emotions felt in the exercise of devout practices? Are not these tears of devotion and other sensible impressions holy love? We have given the answer to this question when speaking of sensible devotion. (1)

(1) Chap. I, Art. III, Sec. III.

SECTION III.—*The Perfection of Divine Love.*

§ I.—*Can man love God perfectly?* (1)

The perfection of charity can be understood in two ways: the first in relation to the object to be loved; the second in relation to the one who loves.

1st. Charity is perfect, relatively to the object to be loved, when the thing is loved as much as it is lovable. Now, God is as worthy of love as he is Good; and as His Goodness is infinite it follows that He is infinitely amiable. But no creature is capable of loving Him in an infinite manner, since all created virtue has its limit. In this regard, therefore, the charity of no creature can be perfect; the only perfect love here is that wherewith God loves Himself as much as He is worthy of being loved.

But one resource is left to the loving soul in its powerlessness, that of humbling itself at the sight of a goodness that merits infinitely more love than she is capable of giving; and since God, nevertheless, loves Himself as much as He is lovable, it will rejoice thereat, uniting the little it can offer to the immense love He bears Himself.

2ndly. Charity will be perfect relatively to the one who loves God, if he loves Him as much as he is capable of loving, as will be explained.

(1) 2a, 2æ, q. 27, a. 3.

§ II.—*Three perfections of Divine Love.* (1)

Man may love God with his whole being and as much as he is capable of doing in three different ways.

The first consists in so loving God that the heart should entirely and always be *actually* uplifted towards Him, and this perfection will be that of our true home; it is not attainable in this life, wherein human infirmity permits not to be always actually thinking of God, nor to tend incessantly towards Him by the movement of love.

This truth may be re-called, if needs be, to certain ambitious and indiscreet souls who desire what is impossible.

A second manner of loving God perfectly consists in this that a person places his whole heart in God *habitually*, so that he thinks of nothing and wishes for nothing contrary to the love that he owes to God, and that he thus puts away from his affection everything that could destroy in him charity, namely, all mortal sin. This perfection, which is of precept, exists in all those who possess charity and are in the state of grace with God. Venial sin is not contrary to it, since this does not destroy the habit of charity.

There is a third way of loving God perfectly that occupies a middle place between the other two: it is that man should make it his whole aim to be in mind and heart entirely

(1) 2a, 2æ, q. 24, a. 8, and q. 1, 84, a. 2.

taken up with God and things divine, leaving aside, everything else in so far as the weakness and the necessities of the present life allow. This perfection of charity, therefore, disengages itself here below, as far as possible, from even lawful things, which by occupying the soul, prevents its actual movement towards God; it strives to exclude from man's affection even the least obstacle which would hinder the total direction of his heart towards the Divine Good.

To this third kind of perfection of charity the evangelical counsels relate as a means to reach it. It may doubtless be found in a person living in the world, and generous souls should be urged to it; but the religious in his state, possesses the proper aids to obtain it and to make constant progress therein. His state itself puts him under the obligation of tending towards it.

§ III.—*The Perfection of Divine Love considered in its act.*

Relatively to its perfection the act of charity may be considered in two ways: either according to its nature or according to its degree.

It is perfect in its nature when it proceeds entirely from the sole motive of charity, without admixture of any other motive. This is also termed the *act of pure love*, whereby we love God exclusively for Himself. Though this charity be perfect, it can always increase

in intensity during the present life, so that its
acts may ever be of a higher perfection.

*The act of charity will be imperfect in its
nature* if God is loved for any other good than
Himself, as His benefits or His rewards. These
inferior motives do not suffice, by themselves,
to produce the act of perfect charity ; but they
dispose our hearts to it: so that, through their
consideration, we easily arrive at loving God
for His goodness as they manifest it to us:
the very chastisement with which He threatens
us or which He does inflict, can dispose us to
the act of charity, when, in order to escape
His justice, we take refuge in the bosom of His
Mercy. (1)

The act of charity is perfect as to its degree,
when, without being perfectly pure in its
nature, it yet makes us prefer God to all other
good, and thus practically love Him above all
things. The necessary mark and the proof of
this charity is the keeping of the commandments, at least as far as the avoidance of mortal sin according to these words of Our Lord:
" If you love Me keep My commandments." (2)

The act of Charity is imperfect as to its degree
and insufficient for salvation, when something
is practically loved more than God or as much
as He is.

Perfect charity as to its nature is that called
by theology *affectivè summa,* supreme on the
side of affection ; perfect charity in degree is

(1) 2a, 2æ, q. 27, a. 3.   (2) John, xiv.

that called *appreciativè summa*, supreme as to appreciation.

In order that the act of charity may justify outside of the sacrament of penance, a man fallen into mortal sin, it is essential that with the desire for the sacrament, his charity should be perfect both as to its degree and as to its nature. Still, this is a consoling truth: for if it sometimes happens to human frailty to fall, a prompt means is at hand, thanks to the Divine Goodness, of recovering God's friendship, whilst waiting for an opportunity to receive the sacrament, and this act of perfect charity is not so difficult as many persons think, especially for the truly Christian soul, who by ardent prayer begs this grace of God.

Some men have taught that divine love, in order to be pure, must tend towards God considered as the sovereign Good in Himself, without any relation to ourselves: so that, say they, he who loves God for his own welfare, has only an *interested* love, which is not pure. These men have not understood what it is to love God: in fact since the very object of love is goodness or that which is good, and since our hearts can become attached only to what we have recognized as good for us, does it not manifestly follow, that to love God is essentially to take complacency in Him and find our good in Him? "What is it to love God gratuitously?" exclaims St. Augustine "It is to love Him for Himself and for nothing else." (1)   And accord-

(1) Quid est gratuitum ? Ipse propter se, et non propter aliud.

ing to St. Alphonsus Liguori, "The desire of possessing God is the proper act of charity, and even the most perfect of all, since the possession of God" is charity consummated.(1)

§ IV.—*Exposition of the great Precept of charity.* (2)

"Thou shalt love the Lord thy God with thy whole heart, and with thy whole mind, and with thy whole soul, and with thy whole strength. (3) This is the greatest and first commandment." (4)

The Angel of the School speaks here with admirable fullness and precision, in order to show in practice the triple perfection of charity just considered; and the religious must remark that the great commandment applies to him as to its third perfection.

Divine love is a movement of the will, as we have said, and it is the will that is here designated by the word *heart*: for as the corporal organ, the heart, is the principle of all the movements of the animal life, so the will,— especially as to its tendency towards its last end which is its proper object,—is the principle of all the movements of the soul and of the spiritual life.

We must well observe and remember that the word *heart,* when speaking of divine love, is a

(1) Desiderium possidendi Deum est actus proprius charitatis, imo omnium perfectissimus; quia possessio Dei est charitas consummata.

(2) 2a, 2æ, q. 44, a. 5.

(3) Deuter. vi, 5.   (4) Matth. xxii, 38.

metaphorical expression used only to express *the will* and its affections; it is never a question of the inferior appetite nor of its sensible emotions.

This is why the great precept of charity is above all addressed to the will since this is the principle of all the movements of the soul. And in fact, as soon as God is Master of the Will, he is Master of the whole man, whence He Himself says to every one of us: "My son, give me thy heart" (1) that is, thy will.

But man has three other principles of his acts which are placed under the command and the impulse of the will: the first is the understanding, here expressed by the word *mind*, *mens;* the second is the inferior and sensitive appetite, rendered by the word *soul, anima,* because it is, in fact, frequently used in Scripture to signify the animal life; the third is the motive power which, through our members, executes exterior actions, and this force of execution is rendered by the words, *power, virtue, strength, fortitudo,* or *virtus,* or *vires.*

The great precept of charity commands us therefore: 1st, to direct to God our whole intention and all the movements of our will: which is really to *love Him with our whole heart;* and this embraces the universality of our interior and free affections;

2nd. Totally to subject to God our understanding and our reason: which is really *to love Him with our whole mind;* therein is contained

(1) Proverbs, xxii, 26.

the homage of faith and of all that relates to
our thoughts, appreciations and judgments;

3rd. To regulate our inferior appetite according to God: which is *to love Him with our whole
soul;* this is our duty in regard to sensibility,
memory and imagination; let us remark the
justness of the word *reguletur;* the will must
hold the curb according to the rule of right
reason, to regulate the inferior appetite and
its passions, as far as depends upon it;

4th. Finally, to watch that all our exterior
actions should be the faithful execution of
God's will, which is *to love Him with all our
strength,* or *with all our virtue* or *all our powers.*
Herein is contained that totality that embraces
the works of God's service whether commanded
by Him or to be done simply at His invitation
and counsel.

See how entire perfection is contained in the
great precept of charity!

But as St. Thomas (1) still says, in Heaven
alone shall it be perfectly accomplished; and
here below, whilst we are on the way, its accomplishment is ever imperfect: for to accomplish the precept perfectly would be to attain
the end proposed by Him Who imposed it.
Yet we still accomplish it, though imperfectly,
when without attaining the legislator's end we
do not turn aside from the order leading thereunto. Thus when the general of an army com-

(1) 2a, 2æ, q. 44, a. 6. This text supplies a refutation of
the Jansenists, and negatives their accusations against
Catholic doctors of theology on this subject of charity.

mands his soldiers to make an attack upon the enemy, they perfectly fulfil the order given who combat in such a manner as to really conquer, which is the end proposed by the general. But those who though combatting, do not attain victory, nevertheless also fulfil, although imperfectly, the order given, so long as they do nothing against military discipline.

The same may be said of the fulfilment of the great precept. It is doubtless God's intention, when imposing it upon man on earth, that he should be totally united to Him. This will take place in Heaven, when, according to the Apostle's expression: "All things will be so subjected to Him that He will be all in all." (1) Yet, it is not imposed uselessly upon those still on the way, though none among them can now attain its perfection: for St. Augustine tells us: "None run as they should, if ignorant of the end towards which they are to run; and how shall they know what is that end if it be not shown to them by any precept." (2)

§ V.—*On a certain totality relating to Divine Love.*

Although nothing be wanting in the exposition just given to thoroughly define the perfection of divine love, it may, however, still be considered under an aspect capable of casting a

(1) I Cor. xv.
(2) Non enim recte curritur, si quo currendum est nesciatur. Quomodo autem sciretur, si nullis præceptis ostenderetur ?

new light upon it. In order to be perfect and
to be lacking in nothing, charity must embrace
a certain *totality* or *universality*, extending to
everything relating to God or belonging to
God.

And what a vast field for the exercise of
Divine Love does not this open to our eyes!
And who should spring forward with more
ardor in this career, than those in the state of
perfection? To love God perfectly and totally,
He must be loved not only in Himself, essence
of Goodness, three Divine persons, and every
one of the infinite attributes of the Divine
Being, but also in all His Divine operations in
the universe. The Incarnate God, Jesus Christ
Our Lord, His Life, His Mysteries, His Name,
His Glory, His Mother, His Saints, etc., are to
be loved; so also all that is done by His Providence, whether in the natural or the supernatural order, especially in us and over us; finally,
God must be loved in all His creatures, in men
especially, His children, Whom He calls *our
neighbor*, and in whose behalf, by a special attention, He has imposed upon us *a second commandment which He declares to be like unto the
first.* (1)

SECTION IV.—*The Effects of Divine Love.*

The effects of Divine Love are of two sorts:
some it produces in the interior of the soul,
the others are manifested by it in exterior
actions.

(1) Matthew, xxii.

§ I.—*The Interior effects of Divine Love.* (1)

1st. Its most immediate effect, when in a soul, is *to produce therein holy affections,* just as it belongs to fire to produce heat. But we have already shown that these affections are properly those of the will, which being free can produce them at all times, even in the absence of sensible affections. Let us add that their intensity, to be judged rightly, is not to be compared with the movements of natural and human love, as for example with maternal love, because the love of God being of an entirely different order, its affection can be true and even more intense, without having the same sensible vehemence.

2ndly. *Divine Love causes Joy:* for joy proceeds from love, either on account of the enjoyment of the good that is loved, or at the sight of a friend's enjoyment of the good that belongs to him.

The principal joy of charity is that rejoicing at the Divine Good, or at the happiness that God possesses in Himself. And this joy in us is incompatible with sadness, just as the good at which it rejoices can have no admixture of evil. This is why the Apostle tells us: "Rejoice in the Lord *always,*" (2) and this in fact can always be done, no matter what evil may beset us in this life. Thousands and thousands of examples of this are given us by the Saints.

Another joy of charity is that rejoicing in the Divine Good according to our participa-

(1) 2a, 2æ, q. 28, 29.   (2) Philip. iv.

tion thereof. For the just man, even in this world, shares in this good, for St. John tells us: "He that abideth in charity, abideth in God and God in Him." (1) And the source of this joy is such that nothing can take it away from him. Sadness may however be mixed with this second joy of charity, on account of the obstacles here below preventing us or those whom we love as ourselves from participating in the Divine Good; these obstacles are sins, spiritual infirmities, the perils of life and the delay of the perfect possession in Heaven.

3dly. *Divine Love causes peace.* Peace is defined by St. Augustine as the tranquillity of order. Now, order within us is often in danger of being troubled, either by the inclinations of the flesh combatting against the spirit, or by those of the will, inclining towards divers objects that it cannot reach simultaneously. Peace then consists in making all these tendencies agree and repose in order. This is an effect produced by charity: for by loving God above all things, it gives to the soul a means of referring all to Him and thus causing all its powers to tend to the one and same end.

4th. *Divine Love causes union with God,* and this in two ways; the first is by the affection of the heart; and love itself is formally this union and bond, since it consists precisely in attachment to God. The second union, which is the effect of the first, comes forth from the

(1) I John, iv.

real drawing nearer of friends, because love causes us to seek the presence of the object loved, as a good which is pleasing and belonging to us. Thus he who truly loves God omits nothing capable of making Him be present to him in every possible way: by communication in prayer, by holy Communion and assiduity in visiting Him in His Sacrament, by recollection and the exercise of the presence of God, finally by the frequent desire of being with Him perfectly as soon as possible in His Kingdom.

5th. *Divine Love even causes a mutual penetration of God and the soul,* according to the Beloved Disciple: "He that abideth in charity, abideth in God and God in him." (1) And this admirable effect of charity is thus explained by St. Thomas.

Mutual penetration takes places both as to the mind and the will. For: 1st, God dwells in the mind of the one who loves Him, insomuch as his thoughts are full of His God; and he dwells in the Divine mind, insomuch, that not content with a superficial knowledge of God, so to say, he penetrates the interior, and strives to attain by meditation as far as he is capable, even to the Divine thoughts, as it is written of the Holy Ghost, who because He is infinite Love, "Searcheth all things, even the deep things of God." (2) 2d, God dwells in the will which loves Him, because He is in its affections, whether it rejoices in Him on

(1) I John, iv.   (1) I Cor. ii.

account of the Goods by Him possessed, or desires itself to possess Him, or strives to procure Him the glory it wishes Him. And the loving will dwells in God's, for the reason that it shows itself inviolably united to this amiable Will by the complete conformity of its affections, its desires, its projects, its determinations and of all its acts.

§ II.—*The exterior effects of divine Love.*

1st. *Love brings forth works.*

Charity is a love of friendship whose interior movement is to wish good to the loved one. Whence it follows that its nature is too liberal and it needs no stimulation in order to act. "If a man," says the Sacred Canticle, "should give all the substance of his house for love, he shall despise it as nothing." (1)

Charity is a friendship between God and man, that is, it creates not only a mutual inclination of hearts between them, but also a mutual benevolence and an ardent deep desire of making a reciprocal communication of their goods. This is why works are necessary on both sides to found, to strengthen and to prove this friendship. Consider how the Divine Friend has shown to you the reality of His love. Count, if you can, its proofs in the order of nature and of grace. Foresee in thought all that He still wills to do for you in the order of glory. But after having fully recognized in heart and mind God's part in

(1) Cant. viii.

His friendship, consider also that which you, the other friend, should in simple justice offer in return by giving Him all that you have and all that you are.

Which are the works in which charity merits more? Are they the most laborious and the most difficult? St. Thomas' answer (1) is that a work may be laborious and difficult in two ways; one on account of the greatness of the act, the other through the fault of the one performing it. In the former case the labor increases the merit; but it belongs to love to diminish the labor without decreasing the merit of the work. In the second case whatever is done without a ready will is found laborious and difficult; the pain then, instead of augmenting the merit of the work, has the effect of lessening it; but it belongs to love to remove or to lighten the labor. This double lesson is worthy of meditation and its application is easy and frequent.

2. *Divine Love produces zeal.* (2)

What is zeal? It is properly the effort made by him who loves, to repulse and to destroy every obstacle contrary to his love.

In general, the more strongly a soul tends towards an object, the more does it strive to move aside the obstacles that impede it. But it is of love, above all, that this is true, which as it grows, repulses with more energy all that is contrary to it, namely, all that fetters it in the pursuit or enjoyment of the good that it

(1) 1a, 2æ, q. 114, a. 4.   (2) 2a, 2æ, q. 28, a. 4.

loves, all that is opposed to the good of its friend. If zeal does not succeed in doing this, it suffers and laments. The exercise of zeal for souls is at the same time that of zeal for the glory of God: for God's great glory consists in being known and loved by His reasonable creatures, and the great practice of charity towards our neighbor is to make him know his supreme Good and to help him to secure its eternal enjoyment.

SECTION V.—*The Second Object of Charity or Love of our Neighbor.*

§ I. *The motive of charity towards our neighbor.*
(1)

1st. Since the reason of our love of our neighbor is the very love we owe to God, it follows therefrom that charity embraces also the love of our neighbor.

We are, in fact, obliged to love that which in our neighbor comes from God, namely the gifts of nature and grace with which He has endowed him, and to love our neighbor that he may himself be in God and God's, by grace in this life and by glory in the next. Whence, it is manifest, that the act by which we love God and our neighbor is the same act of charity, according to kind; and this the Apostle Saint John teaches: "And this commandment we have from God, that he who loveth God, love also his brother." (2)

(1) 2a, 2æ, q. 25, a. 1.   (2) I John, iv, 21.

Love of the neighbor not having God as its
motive, would by that fact alone be useless to
salvation; and it would become culpable if it
rested on the neighbor as on its principal end,
or to the detriment of the love of God.

Such is the great principle of fraternal
charity. How important for Christians, for
religious especially, to comprehend it thoroughly! And how frequently must we return
to it, since self-love makes us so often forget
it!

2d. St. Thomas proposes a question on this
subject, which seems strange at first sight;
but it calls forth an answer that contains several most useful lessons. (1)

Is it more meritorious to love God than to
love our neighbor?

I answer, he tells us, that if each love be
considered separately, divine love is, without
doubt, the more meritorious; for reward is
due to it for its own sake, since the supreme
and final recompense will be the enjoyment of
God towards Whom the movement of that love
tends.

But if we consider divine love according as
a person makes effort to its exclusive exercise,
and the love of the neighbor, according as a
person makes effort to love him for God, then
the love of the neighbor involves the love of
God, whilst the love of God does not contain
the love of the neighbor. Whence we have
the comparison between the perfect love of

(1) 2a, 2æ, q. 27, a. 8.

God which extends to the neighbor, with the
imperfect love of God, because as the holy
Apostle tells us, "God has given this commandment, that he who loves God should also
love his brother;" and in this sense the love
of our neighbor has the pre-eminence.

Thence three practical conclusions spring
forth: first, that he deceives himself, who be-
lieves that he loves God more and merits more
when he withdraws from the exercises of
charity to his neighbor, contrary to his vocation and his state, to apply himself more at
ease to exercises of devotion. Secondly, nevertheless, that it is only from the love of God
that acts of love of our neighbor receive their
merit: whence comes the necessity, as St.
Ignatius so forcibly expresses it, "Of assuring
ourselves before acting, whether the love we experience for our neighbor really springs from the
love of God, so that God may manifestly appear
in our reason for loving our neighbor." (1) The
third lesson is that the love of our neighbor
has one essential condition in order that it
may remain full of the love of God to be
steeped frequently in the special exercises of
Divine Love, which are the spiritual exercises.

(1) Prima regula est, ut amor ille qui me movet, descen-
dat desursum ex amore Dei Domini nostri, ita ut sentiam
primum in me hunc esse propter Deum, et in causo relu-
ceat Deus.   Exer. Spirit. reg. pro eleemosynis.

§ II.— *Exposition of the Second Precept of Charity.*
(1)

"Thou shalt love thy neighbor as thyself."
(2) The words of this precept themselves indicate *the reason* of this love due to our neighbor, and *the manner* in which he should be
loved.

1st. The reason of the love is found in the
word *neighbor*, proximus: this is why we must
love all men with the love of charity, because
they are very near to us, being like us, natural
images of God, like us children of God, and
capable, as well as ourselves, of receiving that
glory to which we are together to be transformed forever in the bosom of God. And
Scripture employs sometimes the word *neighbor*,
now that of *brother*, and again that of *friend*,
to express the same affinity.

2ndly. The manner of loving our neighbor
is expressed by the words: *as thyself*. The
precept does not tell us to love our neighbor
equally to ourselves, but *as ourselves*, and this
in three ways: first, as to the *motive*, we must
love our neighbor for God, since it is thus
that we are bound to love ourselves; and thus
the love we bear him shall be *holy*. Secondly,
as to the *rule* which does not permit us to yield
to the evil desires of others, but only to the
good ones, just as we should yield to our own
desires only in what is upright and good, and
thence our love of our neighbor will be *just*.

(1) 2a, 2æ, q. 44, a. 7.   (2) Matthew, xxii.

Thirdly, as to *the end*, that is, we must not love our brethren for our own interest, but in wishing them good, and hence the love of our neighbor shall be *true*, for to love our neighbor for one's own profit or pleasure, is not really to love him, but ourselves.

§ III.—*Perfect love of our neighbor.* (1)

There are two kinds of perfection with regard to our charity towards our neighbor.

The first, without which charity does not even exist, requires us to remove from our affection all which would destroy the habit of this virtue in ourselves through mortal sin.

The second rises much higher and depends on three things: its extension, its intensity and its effect or exercise.

1st. Charity towards our neighbor will be perfect *in extension*, if we love not only our relations and friends, but also those who are unknown and strangers, and lastly, even our enemies: for, says St. Augustine, "this is the part of God's perfect children." (2)

As much as the perfection of this charity that embraces all men without exception, is worthy of the holy ambition of religious, just as many are the efforts it requires on account of its difficulties. The principal obstacle is not the failings of others or the wrongs done us by them, but it is what we ourselves lay in the way, by forgetting that our neighbor is to

(1) 2a, 2æ, q. 184, a. 2.
(2) Hoc est perfectorum filiorum Dei.

be loved for God and not for what pleases us in him.

2nd. Charity towards our neighbor will be perfect *in intensity*, if, when the occasion comes to test our love for him, we are disposed not to recoil before any sacrifice, and it is thus that for the good of our brethren, not only shall we despise all temporal goods, but be even ready to endure labor, pain, suffering and even death.

3rd. Charity towards our neighbor will be perfect *in its effect* or exercise, if not only all our temporal goods, but also all our spiritual ones are employed for our neighbor's advantage, and lastly, if we devote and spend ourselves in his service, as was done by the great Apostle. (1)

This is fraternal charity such as it is in all those who consecrate their life and works to the welfare of their neighbor; and this perfection is proper to a great number of religious institutes, wherein it becomes the duty and the singular merit of every one of their members.

SECTION VI.—*The Increase of Charity in our Souls.*

§ 1. *Upon whom does this increase depend?* (2)

1st. Charity is a virtue which can have only God for its author: for it is a supernatural

---

(1) But I most gladly will spend and be spent myself for your souls. II Cor. xii, 15.

(2) 2a, 2æ, q. 23, a. 2, and q. 24, a. 2 and 3.

habit intended to perfect the human will, rendering it capable of producing acts of supernatural love, and of producing these with an ever greater facility and promptitude. Charity in us is, moreover, a participation of the infinite charity of God Himself; so that it belongs exclusively to the Holy Ghost to create it and pour it forth in our hearts. (1) Thence it is we call God the life of our soul in the supernatural order: not because He is the formal life of our soul, but because the Holy Ghost infuses charity therein, which is this formal life, as the soul is the life of the body. It is manifest, finally, that since charity has an infinite effect, insomuch as it has the power of justifying the sinner, of uniting him to God and of meriting for him eternal beatitude, that an infinite virtue is required to give it birth in our souls.

Therefore, just as the acquisition of charity is nowise in man's power, so neither as regards its measure or its increase, can it depend either on natural capacity or human virtue. It belongs to the Holy Ghost to augment as well as to produce it in the soul, according to what is written: "The Spirit breatheth where he will;" (2) and again, "Dividing to every one according as he will." (3)

(1) The charity of God is poured forth in our hearts by the Holy Ghost, who is given to us. Romans, v, 5.

(2) John, iii, 8.

(3) But all these things one and the same Spirit worketh, dividing to every one according as he will. I Cor. xii, 11.

2nd. It is, however, true, that God demands our preparation and efforts in order to give us the first infusion or an increase of charity, and this is the meaning of these words of Our Lord: "He delivered to his servants his goods, ... to every one according to his proper ability." (1) But even this preparation and these efforts are forestalled by the Holy Ghost, as Faith teaches, who excites our will more or less according to His good pleasure: so that it is always He, according to the Apostle's expression, "Who hath made us worthy to be partakers of the lot of the Saints." (2)

3d. We must conclude therefrom, first, that the means is the same whether to increase charity in us and consequently perfection, or to acquire and preserve it, that is: we must address ourselves to God by prayer; secondly, that we must also do our share, with the aid of grace, by removing obstacles and by co-operating with the action of the Holy Ghost. Would to God our co-operation were always what it might and should be! "There are few souls" says St. Ignatius, "perfectly faithful in appreciating the gifts they receive, and who reach the degree of charity and perfection to which God desired to raise them."

§ II.—*What is the increase of Charity?*

1st. Charity increases in our soul in that it becomes more intense in order to produce more fervent acts by the will; and when God aug-

---

(1) Matthew, xxv, 14, 15.　　　(2) Coloss. i, 12.

ments it in us, He makes us participate to a greater degree in resemblance to the Holy Ghost who is Charity, uncreated and infinite.

2nd. Charity can increase in a soul until the end of the present life. In fact, the reason why we are called *travellers* is because we must travel towards God, who is the last term of our beatitude. And in this journey, we advance the more as we approach God the more, not, as St. Augustine tells us, by the steps of the body, but by the affections of the soul. And it is charity that causes us to approach God in this manner, by more and more attach-ing us to Him. It then belongs to charity to have the power of ever increasing in this life; otherwise we should stop on our journey. Therefore St. Paul calls charity a road: "And I show unto you yet a more excellent way."(1)

A touching reflection may be made here: if envy could find a place in Heaven, the Saints would certainly envy us this: their charity is no longer susceptible of growth as ours is here below; although perfect in its degree, it might have been so in a superior degree by the aug-mentation they might have merited on earth.

3rd. Charity can increase indefinitely in this life. For it is impossible to assign to it any limit, whether as regards its *form*, which is a participation of infinite charity, or as to its *cause*, who is God Himself, Whose virtue has no bounds, or as to the soul receiving it since the increase of charity is accompanied by

(1) I Cor. xii.

increased aptitude for further augmentation. Charity, whilst becoming thus ever more perfect, tends to one end and term; but this end is not in the present life, but only in the life to come. Then exclaims St. Augustine: "However long we have lived, however far we have walked and advanced, none can say: It is enough for me. To say that is to remain on the way and not to know how to arrive. There where you have said: "It is enough, there you have stopped." (1)

§ III. *Does Charity increase in us at every act of it that we perform?* (2)

1st. The Angelic Doctor gives a negative answer, which he makes clear with this comparison.

The spiritual increase of charity may be compared, in some manner, with what takes place corporally in the animal or the plant. Here the increase is not continual: nature operates for some time by disposing to augmentation, without causing any actual growth; then comes the moment in which it produces the effect for which it had made preparation and then it really augments the plant or animal.

It is thus with charity; every act of it that we perform does not always actually increase

(1) Quantumcumque vixerimus, aut profecerimus, nemo dicat: Sufficit mihi; qni enim hoc dixerit, remansit in via, non novit pervenire. Ubi dixerit: Sufficit, ibi hæsit.

(2) 2a, 2æ, q. 24, a. 6.

it, but each disposes it to increase by rendering the will more prompt to the performance of another act; and the aptitude thus increasing, the person by this comes to some act of love more intense, by which he strives to advance in charity and it is then actually augmented.

The reason which proves that charity does not increase by every one of its acts, is that an effect cannot exceed the efficacy of its cause; and it sometimes happens that an act of charity is made with tepidity and remissness; it is manifest that this act, far from conducting to a greater charity, rather disposes the soul to a lesser one.

2ndly. Two remarks may be made here: first, that this doctrine of St. Thomas in no wise contradicts the definition of the Council of Trent, *that man in a state of grace merits through the good works that he performs an increase of grace*, (1) for the holy Doctor textually professes this truth by thus explaining it: "As every act of charity merits eternal life, not as obtainable at once, but in its proper time with perseverance; so it also merits augmentation of charity, not at the very moment of its occurrence, but when the person strives to obtain it." The second remark is that these acts that are performed with tepidity and remissness, these tepid prayers and communions multiplied by certain persons instead of

(1) Si quis dixerit . . . . . hominem justificatum, bonis operibus quæ ab eo fiunt . . . non vere mereri augmentum gratiæ . . . . anathema sit. Sess. VI, can. 32.

increasing charity in them, have as their only result to dispose to a successive decrease of it. This is a serious lesson for souls cowardly in God's service.

§ IV.—*Directions to be followed in order to progress in charity.* (1)

As everything has a beginning, a middle, and an end, so there are three degrees to charity : that which is beginning, that which progresses, and that which has reached its perfection.

St. Augustine, comparing charity to a human body, warns us that when it is born in a soul it must be nourished in order to live; then it must be strengthened until it has reached its perfect development. (2) According to these three principal and successive degrees, man must especially apply himself to different cares : the first is that of avoiding sin, the second, exercising himself in virtue, and the third, striving for union with God.

In fact, the soul newly born to the life of grace must make its principal care be the avoidance of sin and the striving against the concupiscences that tend to move it contrary to charity. This is the task of *beginners,* in whom charity must be nourished and sustained that it may not become corrupted and lost.

(1) 2a, 2æ, q. 24, a. 9.
(2) Charitas, cum fuerit nata, nutritur; cum fuerit nutrita, roboratur; cum fuerit roborata, perficitur; cum autem ad perfectionem venerit, dicit: Cupio dissolvi et esse cum Christo.

These nourishments and these means are, among others, the exercise of the fear of God, temperance, mortification, the diligent use of examination of conscience and recourse to the sacraments.

Then comes a second state of charity in which the principal care should be to advance in well-doing, and to strengthen charity by the acquisition of virtues: this is the task of those called *proficientes*, that is, of those who advance by the growth of charity in them. Meditation and imitation of the virtues of Jesus Christ and His Saints are their great and efficacious means.

There is, finally, a third state of charity, that of a certain perfection already acquired, in which the soul, when it is conscious of having reached it, can and should apply itself principally to the exercises of union with God: for it belongs to the *perfect* to enjoy God, and, as St. Paul did, "to sigh for their release that they may be with Jesus Christ." (1)

It is thus that in a bodily movement, there is a first degree which consists in getting away from the starting point; then a second degree by which we approach the term; and finally a third degree in which rest is found at the term itself.

Those in whom charity begins, have doubtless the intention of advancing, but their principal study should be resistance to the sins

(1) Having a desire to be dissolved and to be with Christ. Philipp. i, 23.

whose aggression molests them most. Afterwards feeling the necessity of these combats
less, they may with more assurance apply themselves to their advancement. In this way they
will act as did the Israelites who rebuilt the
City of Jerusalem, in the time of Esdras: (1)
with one hand they will raise the edifice of
virtues, but with the other they will still hold
the sword in case of the attack by the enemy.
The perfect, on their side, never give up the
work of their spiritual progress, since charity
here below is ever imperfect, and always needs
to increase, (2) and they even cannot entirely
neglect the enemies that often cause their
attacks to be felt and that are ever to be feared.
Their principal study, nevertheless, is application to union with God; this they do, not by
a lazy quietude nor to the neglect of their
duties, but by the perfect intention of love
when they have anything to do, by the exercise of the presence of God, by the contemplation of His perfections and of His works, by
the care of loving Him in all His creatures and
all His creatures in Him. And although the
others seek this union with God, yet these
always feel more solicitude both in putting sin
aside and in practicing and advancing in virtue.

It can be seen that these three degrees of the
spiritual life in charity are nothing else than

(1) Esdras, iv.
(2) Perfectio viæ non est perfectio simpliciter, et ideo
semper habet quo crescat. 2a, 2æ, q. 24, a. 8, ad 3.

what is also called *the purgative, the illumina-tive* and *the unitive way;* and the Angelic Doctor shows most usefully the manner in which these three ways must be understood in practice.

SECTION VII.—*The Decrease and the loss of Charity.* (1)

1st. St. Thomas teaches that the habit of charity in a soul can be diminished *directly* neither by the cessation of acts nor by venial sin.

Not by the cessation of acts, since charity is not a natural habit of man, but the work of God in him.

Nor by venial sin, since that sin is only an irregularity touching the means, not attacking charity which refers to the end. Morever, he who sins in a secondary matter does not deserve a principal punishment, and God does not turn more from man than man turns from God by his sin: which would happen, if, for having failed as to the means, we were to suffer loss in charity which unites to the end.

Hence it is to be concluded that charity can-not be directly diminished by man, if con-sidered as to its substance, the degree of union established between God and the soul, and the corresponding merit for eternal life.

But *indirectly* a person can weaken charity in himself by preparing its ruin both by venial sin and by the cessation of acts. Venial sins

(1) 2a, 2æ, q. 24, a. 10.

prepare its ruin by disposing to mortal sin by
which it is destroyed. The cessation of acts
of charity is also a preparation for its loss, in
so far, that the habit of charity becomes less
prompt to produce its acts; and then a vicious
habit can easily introduce itself into the soul,
and prevail therein by some mortal sin.

St. Gregory the Great cites, on this subject,
the sad example of his aunt Gordianne, who
had vowed her virginity to God, and who, by
daily decrease, at last failed in her sworn
pledge, and was lost. (1)

It is clear, that properly to understand the
meaning of all of this passage of St. Thomas,
the substance of charity must be distinguished
from its ardor in promptitude to produce acts.
This ardor is but too much exposed to grow
cold and to decrease by the commission of
venial sins and by laxity.

1I.—In Heaven, wherein God is seen face to
face and in His essence, the infinite Goodness
and Beauty by manifesting themselves to the
Blessed so ravish their affection, that they can
no longer lose charity. But on earth, where
we see God only through the veil of faith, we
are always exposed to the misfortune of losing
charity through sin.

One single mortal sin suffices to destroy it in
man's heart: so that he who possessed through

(1) Cœpit paulatim a calore amoris intimi per quotidiana
decrementa tepescere: unde factum est ut postmodum oblita dominici timoris, oblita pudoris, oblita reverentiæ, oblita consecrationis, conductorem agrorum suorum matri-
monio duxerit.

it the life of grace and the merit of life eternal, becomes in one moment worthy of eternal death.

In the case of acquired virtues, a single contrary act does not destroy the virtuous habit, for that a succession of repeated acts is needed, which weaken it little by little, and finally by effacing and corrupting it entirely. But charity, being an infused virtue, depends upon the action of God who has poured it forth and preserves it in the soul; now this action of God may be compared to the manner in which the sun illumines the atmosphere; just as light would then cease to exist in the atmosphere, as soon as an obstacle would arise to the sun's action, so charity ceases to exist in the soul of the just man, as soon as an obstacle intercepts the divine influence. Every mortal sin is manifestly this obstacle, since as by it man prefers his sin to God's friendship; that friendship which requires that the friends should have the same will, is broken, and at that moment the habit of charity is lost and immediately destroyed.

It should, besides, he remarked that man may lose charity in two ways: one direct and the other indirect. He loses it directly by his formal contempt of it, which happens when he sins through malice and then it is more difficult to regain. He loses it indirectly when he sins through surprise or when carried away by passion. It is in this way that St. Peter lost charity, but he recovered it promptly through penance. Whence we see that the soul suffers much more harm from a sin of malice than from one of frailty.

III. *On the Sins of religious.* (1)

St. Thomas asks the following question: When offending God in a like matter does a religious sin more grievously than a secular? And behold his answer: If the religious sins through contempt, against his vows or by giving scandal to another, his sin is more grievous than that of a secular; but it is the contrary if it is only through ignorance or infirmity that he sins.

In fact, when sinning through malice and contempt, his sin is more grievous, since he shows more ingratitude towards the Divine Bounty which has granted to him the signal favor of raising him to the state of perfection. And the Lord complains of this by His Prophet: "What is the meaning that my beloved hath wrought much wickedness in my house." (2)

It is clear that if the religious dare sin against his vows his sin is greater, since it contains a double malice, as has been already shown.

If he give scandal by his sin, the religious may be and generally is more guilty, because his life attracts the attention of a greater number of persons.

But when the religious fails neither through contempt nor by malice, but only through weak-

(1) 2a, 2æ, q. 186, a. 10.   (2) Jerem. xi, 15.

ness or ignorance, and without scandal or violation of his vow, he sins less than a secular, in this sense, that his sin is less injurious, because, if venial, it is as it were absorbed by the multitude of good works that he performs; and if mortal the religious gets rid of it more easily. The facility has two causes:

The first is that his intention is habitually upright towards God; therefore if it suffers a momentary interruption, he has no trouble to make it resume its direction and to repair the injury that has befallen it. This is Origen's thought in explanation of the words of the Psalm: "When the just shall fall he shall not be bruised, for the Lord putteth his hand under him." (1) The unjust, says Origen, when he has sinned has no repentance, and knows not how to get himself clear from his sin; whilst the just knows how to correct himself without delay: like him who having said of His Divine Master: *I know not that man*, had need only of one look from the Lord to weep bitterly; like him also who, having seen a woman from the roof-top and allowed his heart to be carried away, was soon able to say: *I have sinned, O my God, and done iniquity in Thy Presence.*

The second reason is that the religious who falls finds in his brethren a help to arise, according to these words of the Wise Man: "If one fall, he shall be supported by the other: Woe

(1) Psalm xxxvi, 24.

to him that is alone, for when he falleth, he hath none to lift him up!" (1)

The just sin with difficulty through contempt, and this is why, in case they do fall, they rise easily. But when they reach the point of sinning through contempt, they become very wicked and the most incorrigible of all. Thence those terrible words of St. Augustine: "Since I have begun to serve God, I have found by experience, that as there are scarcely any Christians better than those who do good in religious houses, so there are no worse than those who abandon themselves to evil therein."

Would it not be well, when speaking of the sins of religious, to set forth the Angelical Doctor's doctrine in its two parts?

SECTION VIII.—*Charity in its relation to the other virtues.*

Charity is termed and is in fact the *form*, the *mother*, the *foundation*, the *bond* and the *end* of all the other virtues: whence we see how it is also by excellence their queen, and in how many ways it is essential to religious perfection. (2)

I. Charity is *the form of the other virtues*, not if they be considered as to their own species, since every virtue has it special form, arising from the object upon which it is exercised; but in this sense that charity must impress its own form upon them, without which no virtue

(1) Eccl. iv, 10.　　　　(2) 2a, 2æ, q. 23, a. 7.

would merit the name of true virtue, taking that word in its pure and absolute acceptation. (1)

In fact all virtue is essentially a habit having good as its object; and good exists principally in its end: for means are good only insomuch as they refer to the end. This is why, as there are two sorts of ends, one near and the other our last, so there are two kinds of goods, one near or special, the other final, supreme and universal. The final good for man, that which should embrace all others, is the possession of God, according to these words of the Psalmist: "It is good for me to stick close to my God;" (2) and man can attain this Good only through charity.

As to the near, secondary and particular good of man, it can be of two kinds; one which is a true good, in that it serves as a means to attain the supreme good and the last end; the other which is only apparent and not real, because it turns away from the final good. Whence it evidently follows that no virtue is true unless directed by charity to the Supreme good and of the last end of man.

If we call virtue that limiting itself to some special good, without being referred to the final good by charity, in that case, the virtue may, it is true, have some reality; nevertheless, should this special good be only apparent and not real, then will the virtue be also

(1) Simpliciter vera virtus, sine charitate, esse non potest.
(2) Psalm lxxvii, 28.

only apparent. "Thus," says St. Augustine: "We cannot call true virtues neither the prudence of the avaricious, which knows the secret of becoming richer, nor their justice which respects the property of others only through fear of punishment, nor their temperance which represses in them the sumptuous tastes of sensuality, nor finally, their strength which, according to the saying of the poet, makes them fly poverty across sea, rocks and flames." (1) If this particular good is in fact, real, as the care of relieving the unfortunate, filial piety, fidelity to one's word, there then shall be some reality in the virtue, but it will remain imperfectly true so long as it does not refer to the final and perfect good. Whence we must still conclude that in the *absolute* signification of the word virtue, there is no true virtue without charity.

Would to God that all men understood this fundamental truth! Would to God, that religious themselves made a better application of it to every one of their actions! Where charity is wanting, every virtue, if virtue it is, is only a grovelling virtue which never rises from earth; whilst with charity and through charity, the most humble virtue has the power of ascending even into Heaven and of meriting the Supreme Good.

II. "Charity is *the mother of all virtues*," because its proper object and the end to which

(1) Per mare pauperiem fugiunt, per saxa, per ignes. Horat., lib. 1, epist. 1.

it aspires being the possession of God Himself,· its desire of attaining Him ever more perfectly, causes it *to conceive* acts of the other virtues in the interest of its own end ; it *brings them forth* when it commands the will to produce them. Thence is it that the Apostle attributes them all to it. "Charity is patient," he tells us, "it is kind: charity envieth not, it is not puffed up, etc." (1)

This is why that the more charity increases in a soul, the more fruitful it becomes in acts of *all the* virtues, putting them into exercise and exacting labor and activity from them. On the contrary, if virtues produce little, it is that charity is weak and languid; and a manifest proof of its total absence is the idleness of the other virtues.

III. *Charity is the foundation of virtues.*

These virtues are said to be the foundation of all the others, namely : humility, faith and charity. We shall see in what sense this name of foundation suits them each.

As to humility and faith, this is St. Thomas' exposition. (2)

Just as the well-ordered collection of man's virtues is compared to an edifice, so the first requisite to this spiritual construction is compared to the foundation, by which a material edifice must be begun. Now, the virtues of a person are much less his own work than God's to Whom it belongs to implant them in us and to make them increase. Whence it follows

(1) I Cor. xiii, 4, 5.   (2) 2a, 2æ, q. 161, a. 5.

that, in what affects the virtues, a thing may. be called the first or foundation in two differant ways: one direct and the other indirect.

1st. The thing which is to be *indirectly* the first or foundation with regard to the virtues, is that which is to remove the obstacles to the divine action within us.

It is thus that humility occupies the first place, by chasing pride which God resists (1) and by putting down the swellings of that vice, it presents a soul submissive and generously open to divine grace. (2) It is, then, in this sense and in this manner that humility is the foundation of the spiritual edifice of all the virtues, according to these words of St. Augustine: "You wish to elevate a great structure, think first of the foundation of humility; and the higher the building is to be the deeper must the foundation be dug."

2ndly. The thing which should be *directly* the first or foundation in reference to the virtues, is that by which we are to approach towards God, the Lord of virtues. And it is by faith that man comes near to God, as taught by the Apostle: "For he that cometh to God, must believe that He is." (3) And it is in this sense that faith is the foundation of all the virtues, in even a more noble manner than humility.

(1) For God resisteth the proud. I Peter, v, 5.
(2) Weigh well these strong words: Prœbet hominem subditum et patulum divinæ gratiæ.
(3) Credere enim oportet accedentem ad Deum quia est. Heb. XI, 6.

3rdly. But St. Paul also calls charity a foundation. "You are," he tells the Christians, "rooted and founded in charity," (1) because like to a foundation and a root, charity, in fact sustains and nourishes all the other virtues. It is their living and life-giving foundation, as the root is this to all the branches of the tree; which is even a more elevated manner of being a foundation than that of humility and faith. Whence we have those beautiful words of St. Gregory, Pope: "All that God commands to men He makes it rest on charity alone: for just as the different branches of a tree come solely from the root, so that divers virtues are all the product of charity; and the branch of good works retains none of its verdure if it does not remain united to the root of charity." (2)

IV. Charity is *the bond of the other virtues.* (3) Therefore, after having told us that charity is to be possessed above all, the Apostle immediately adds that it is the bond of perfection. (4)

In fact, as the other virtues are necessary to the completion of perfection, as has been elsewhere explained, (5) so it belongs to charity

(1) Ephes. iii, 17.

(2) Quidquid præcipitur, in sola charitate solidatur: ut enim multi arboris rami ex una radice prodeunt, sic multæ virtutes ex una charitate generantur; nec habet aliquid viriditatis ramus boni operis, si non manet in radice charitatis.

(3) 2a, 2æ, q. 184, a. 1, and q. 65, a. 3.

(4) But above all these things have charity, which is the bond of perfection. Coloss. iii, 14.

(5) As above—Ch. II, art. III, sec. I.

not only to produce and to feed them, but also
to bind them all together as a bunch in perfect
unity. The reason of this is that charity is the
principle of all the good works by which man
must arrive at his last end; and for this it is
necessary that it should be accompanied by
all the other virtues which produces the diverse
kinds of good works.

For this reason, in the just man the moral
virtues have among themselves not only the
connection which is according to prudence, but
also that other connection which is according
to charity. Kept together by this bond of
charity, as strong as it is soft, all the virtues
remain with it in the soul, and none can be
missing so long as it itself is present; and
through it, moreover, all are in a harmo-
nious unity, so that no act of one virtue can
interfere with that of another. Such is perfection or sanctity according to Christianity,
and we know by the history of the canoniza-
tion of Saints, that in order to declare authen-
tically its existence in a Christian, the Catholic Church exacts the irrefragable proof that he
possessed this union of all the virtues in
charity, even to an heroic degree.

V.—Charity is, finally, *the end of all the
other virtues*, (1) because it keeps them under
its orders, and its direction to make them advance towards its end. All are its instruments
and servants. Some it employs in removing
the obstacles which would impede its union

(1) 2a, 2æ, q. 23, a. 8.

with God : such as strength, patience and abnegation, with all the others derived therefrom,
humility,. temperance, mortification, modesty,
etc. Others it employs more directly in exercising itself either towards God or the neighbor;
as faith, hope, religion, justice, zeal, etc.

But among all the virtues that it employs to
tend towards its perfection, there are three
that call for the special attention of religious :
these are the three virtues consecrated by the
vows of religion, poverty, chastity and obedience. We shall now consider more fully in
the following article their relation to charity.

———

ARTICLE IV.

THE MEANS OF PERFECTION FOUND IN THE RELIGIOUS STATE.

These means are of two kinds : some principal, others secondary ; some most efficaciously
used by charity for its own perfection ; others
giving their concourse to the first for the same
end, and being also of great utility to the perfection of the other virtues ; it is clear that it
is a question here of *vows* and of *rules.*

SECTION I.—*The Vows, the Principal means of
Perfection.* (1)

I. The religious state is *a discipline,* that is,
*a school in which one learns, and a career in which
one is exercised,* to the end of acquiring the per-

(1) 2a, 2æ, q. 186, a. 3, 4, 5, 6.

fection of charity. Now, for this four things are necessary.

In the first place, it is necessary, that voluntary poverty be practised in the religious state. I speak here of that poverty that consists in the effectual spoliation of temporal goods. For the perfection of charity exacts that man should totally disengage his affection from terrestrial things, to be able to make it trend entirely towards God, according to what is said by St. Augustine: "Lord he loves Thee too little, who loves something with Thee, which he loves not for Thee:" (1) and again, "the food of charity is the spoil taken from cupidity; charity is perfect when cupidity no longer remains." (2) But experience teaches that he who possesses temporal goods is much exposed to attach his heart to them, as is energetically expressed by the same St. Augustine: "Wealth clings much more to the heart when possessed, than when only desired. For whence comes it that the young man in the Gospel withdrew with sadness, if not because he possessed great wealth? It is one thing not to desire to incorporate what is outside of ourselves, and quite another to pluck out what is already within us. In the first case it is like a foreign body that is removed; in the second it is as if our

(1) Minus te amat, qui tecum amat aliquid quod non propter te amat.

(2) Nutrimentum charitatis est imminutio cupiditatis; perfectio, nulla cupiditas.

members were undergoing amputation." (1)
This is why evangelical poverty is the first foundation to be laid, when it is a question of acquiring the perfection of charity, Our Lord, Himself having said: "If thou wilt be perfect, go, sell what thou hast, and give it to the poor." (2)

In the second place the practice of continence is necessary: first, because even were carnal pleasures lawful, they are a great obstacle to the perfect aim of man's affections towards God; and, next, because the same may also be said of the cares imposed by the government and the temporal necessities of a family, as St. Paul tells us: "He that is with a wife is solicitous for the things of this world, and he is divided." (3)

In the third place, obedience is above all necessary, according to Our Lord's counsel: "If you wish to be perfect . . . come, follow me." Now, what most calls forth our imitation in the life of Our Divine Model, is His obedience, as St. Paul remarks: "Becoming obedient unto death." (4) And in fact, let us recall the principle already laid down, that the religious state is an apprenticeship and a career having as its end the acquisition of perfection. But all persons who are learning and who practice in order to become skilful, have

(1) Terrena diliguntur arctius adepta, quam concupita. . . . . Aliud est enim nolle incorporare quæ desunt, aliud jam incorporata divellere. Illa enim velut extranea repudiantur, ista vero velut membra præscinduntur.
(2) Matt. xix: (3) I Cor. vii, 33.   (4) Philip. ii, 8.

need of some one to teach them and to direct
them, as disciples under a master. This is
why it is necessary for religious to be under
the direction and the authority of some one
in the whole government of their religious life,
which is done by means of obedience: whence
Canon law says, that "the life of a religious is a
life of subjection and a school." (1)

In the fourth place, it is necessary that a
person should impose on himself these three
things under the obligation of a vow, in order
to be by that means entirely given up, in a
fixed and constant manner, to the perfection
of charity, according to these words of St.
Gregory: "To vow to the Lord all the goods
of fortune, all those of the body, and all those
of the mind, is the perfect sacrifice of the holocaust." (2) Moreover, as the perfection of life
consists in consecrating it entirely to the
Divine worship, this perfection requires that
we should effectually present to God all that
we desire to consecrate to him. But man cannot present to God his whole life in one act,
since that life elapses successively; the only
means to offer the whole effectually is by the
obligation of the perpetual vow, by which the
entire life is bound.

II. The same St. Thomas thus sums up all
that the three vows of religion do for the perfection of charity: (3)

(1) Monachorum vita subjectionis habet verbum et dis-
cipulatus.

(2) Cum quis omne habet, omne quod sepit, omnipotenti
Deo voverit, holocaustum est.

(3) 2a, 2æ, q. 186, a. 7.

The religious state may be considered under
three aspects: the first, as an exercise by which
perfection is aimed at; the second, insomuch
as it frees the human heart from exterior solici-
tudes; the third, as a holocaust, wherein all is
given to God without reserve. Under this threefold aspect, the religious state furnishes fully
what is required for the perfection of charity.

1st. It removes the interior obstacles preventing a total trend of our affections towards
God. These obstacles are three: cupidity for
wealth is the first, and the vow of poverty removes it; concupiscence of the flesh is the
second, and is excluded by the vow of chastity;
the disorder of the will is the third, and the
vow of obedience makes it disappear, by plac-
ing our will under the direction of God Himself, commanding by the superior.

2ndly. It removes the exterior obstacles:
for the solicitude of the world disquiets the
soul chiefly in three things, one relating to
the care and expenditure of temporal goods,
another, to the government of a family, and the
third to the disposition of one's own acts; these
three sources of inquietude are taken away by
the three vows of religion, according to the
desire formed by St. Paul for perfect Christians:
"I would have you to be without solicitude."
(1)

3d. Under the third aspect, the religious
state does more then remove obstacles; it is

(1) I Cor. vii.

already the exercise of perfect charity: for it
is a holocaust, as St. Gregory has said, to
sacrifice to God all that we possess. Now, man
may possess three kinds of goods: wealth,
which he sacrifices to God by voluntary poverty; the goods of the body, of which he deprives himself for His love by the vow of continence, and those of the soul which he offers
Him totally by the vow of obedience, since he
sacrifices his will by which he makes use of all
the powers and habits of his soul.

III. Two objections may here present themselves to the mind: one against poverty, the
other against religious obedience.

This is the first: almsgiving is a work as
agreeable to God and as sweet to the heart!
Well! this is excluded by voluntary poverty,
and once I shall have despoiled myself of
everything, this merit and consolation can
no longer be mine. This is the pretext sometimes used by the enemy of salvation, to turn
away a tender soul from religious perfection.

It must be said, answers St. Thomas, that
the renunciation of temporal goods when compared with almsgiving, is a universal good
compared with a particular good, and as the
sacrifice of holocaust, in which the entire victim is offered, compared with the other sacrifices in which a part is reserved. (1) This is
why St. Jerome, refuting the error of Vigil-
antius, speaks in these terms: "It is a good
thing to distribute one's goods to the poor suc-

(1) 2a, 2æ, q. 186, a. 3, ad 6m, a. 5, ad 5m, and a. 6, ad 3m.

cessively; but it is better still to give all at once to follow Jesus Christ, and after having cut off all terrestrial solicitude, to live poor with Jesus Christ." Add still the sacrifice of the heart itself so full of abnegation and humility, when a religious is reduced to say to the unfortunate, stretching out a hand to him: "Alas, I have no longer anything to give!"

The objection against religious obedience is this: spontaneous services are those most agreeable to God; but once the vow of obedience has been made, spontaneity gives place to necessity; and the same may be said of the two other vows, which take away thenceforth the merit of spontaneous privation.

It must be said, still answers St. Thomas, that the necessity of constraint renders the act involuntary and consequently without merit. But such is not the necessity ensuing from the vow of obedience: for man even *then* remains entirely master of his will, and acts because he wishes to obey, although the thing commanded, if considered in itself, might perhaps otherwise be not according to his inclina-nation. And it is just because he has imposed upon himself for God's sake, the necessity of doing things not pleasing to him, that his actions are more agreeable to God, even when meaner than those he himself would have chosen: because man can give to God nothing greater than for His sake to subject his own will to that of another.

The same must be said of the necessity imposed by the two other vows.

For among the goods which can be renounced is his own liberty, which is the one most cherished by man. This is why the free withdrawal of one's power of thenceforth acting contrary to poverty and perfect chastity is the use of liberty which is most agreeable to God. Whence St. Augustine thus speaks to the religious: "Repent not of having bound yourself by vows; but rather rejoice no longer to be able to do what would have been allowed you to your detriment. Happy necessity which obliges us to do what is the better!" (1)

SECTION II.—*Secondary means of perfection—the Rules.*

The "Catechism of the Vows" indicates in a few words (2) what help the rules are to make the religious tend to perfection. But several useful explanations are still to be given on this subject.

I. A *rule*, in Latin *regula* and in Greek *canon*, is an architectural instrument known by all. Indispensable for material constructions, the rule is no less so for the spiritual edifice of the virtues and perfection.

The essential quality of a rule is to be straight: *regula*, according to St. Isidore, is as if we said

(1) Non te vovisse pœniteat, imo gaude jam tibi non licere quod cum tuo detrimento licuisset. Felix necessitas quæ in meliora compellit!

(2) Part 1st, ch. 2.

rectula, on account of the rectitude inherent in
it; and Seneca the philosopher judiciously observes "that it is outraging rectitude to act
according to a rule that we have ourselves
bent," (1) beautiful maxim showing wherein
lies supreme disorder, irremediable cause of all
the others. The rule, says St. Gregory, suffers
neither addition, nor curtailment; otherwise
it loses its very property of rule, (2) in a word,
if rectitude is wanting to the rule, it misleads
the workman, it spoils the work, and it even
compromises the solidity of the edifice. This
is why when it is question of a rule of religious
life the approbation of the Church is necessary,
to certify that it is truly straight; and again
this is why it is so important to an institute
that its approved rule should not be tampered
with, but that its rectitude should be lovingly
respected by everybody.

II.—The rule in the mason's hand makes
him know if the wall he raises is even and
perpendicular: in order that seeing a stone too
far in he may push it forward, and seeing one
projecting he may bring it back; this comparison is made by St. Gregory (3) and it is applicable continually in the work of perfection.
Rule comes from the word *regere,* because it is

(1) Regulam si flectas, quidquid ex illa mutaveris, inju-
ria est recti.

(2) Regula nec addi sibi quidquam, nec demi sustinet;
alioquin hoc ipsum quod regula est, amittit ac perdit.

(3) Ut si lapis intus est, foras emittatur; si autem exte-
rius prominet, interius revocetur.

destined to *direct* and to *correct* (1); these are its two essential functions: it directs in the moral order by showing what is to be either done or avoided; it corrects by recalling to *rectitude* whatever strays from it and by reproving and punishing *wrong*.

III. By *the Rule of an institute* is meant the collection of all the prescriptions concerning it: and here two kinds of elements are to be distinguished, some more essential and of a first order, the others complementary and of a second order. He, says St. Thomas, who professes the rule, or who rather promises to live according to the rule, does not engage himself by vow to keep all the particulars in the rule; but he vows to live the regular life which consists essentially in keeping the three vows. For in a law some things are proposed not under the form of precept obliging under pain of sin, but by way of *ordination* or of direction obliging only to some penalty if not observed. However, as the religious has promised to live according to the rule, that is, to strive to form his life upon it as upon a model presented to him, he would violate this engagement and sin even grievously, if he were to despise the rule in any point whatever; and this contempt exists when the transgression proceeds. precisely from this—that the will refuses to submit to the rule. But an infraction of some point of the rule through some other particu-

(1) Regula a regendo, id est, dirigendo et corrigendo, quia vel rectum dirigit, vel distortum corrigit.

lar cause, such as anger, sloth, etc., is no sin of contempt; yet it is to be remarked that little by little these infractions engender contempt when they become frequent. (1)

IV. We sometimes distinguish *the Rule* in the singular, and *the Rules* in the plural.

The Rule, considered according to this distinction, is exclusively the exposition of the most substantial points of the institute that have been presented for the approbation of the Church. Thus understood, the rule is what gives existence to a religious body, when it is approved and put into execution.

But this rule, on account of its brevity, requires further developments according to its spirit: thence *the rules of detail* or *constitutions*, either those regarding the body of the institute, or those to be observed personally by the members.

These rules, as their very name expresses, must always verify the idea of rectitude, and this is why the authorization of the Church is necessary to the founders or heads of institutes, to be able to make and to impose them. The Church even generally wishes still to examine them and to add its formal approbation, the more to warrant their rectitude.

The Holy See no longer uses the name *Rule* to designate the collected constitutions of any pious institute approved by it. That name is reserved for the ancient orders, under whose rule divers more recent congregations have

(1) 2a, 2æ, q. 186, a. 9.

placed themselves: the Rule of St. Basil, the Rule of St. Benedict, of St. Augustine, of St. Francis, etc.

V. Among the Rules or constitutions which relate personally to the members of an institute, there are two sorts which it is important to distinguish:

Some have for object the formation of each religious according to the spirit proper to the institute: these are *the Rules of the interior life.* Therein are laid down the principles from which every member is to draw a multitude of practical consequences, in order to tend to the positive perfection of his vows and to the perfection of virtues according to his vocation. It is to be remarked that these rules rather prescribe a tendency, efforts and an ever growing progress, than utter a command or a prohibition to particular acts. Thus, although it is the duty of all to endeavor to follow their direction, nevertheless, for the most part, they are not and even cannot be observed by all equally; but there are very different degrees for individuals, and every one practices them according to his own power, to the grace given him, to his actual fervor, and to the progress he has already made in perfection.

The object of the other rules is discipline or the exterior part of common life: this is the reason why they are generally called *common rules.* They prescribe or forbid acts produced exteriorly; and their end is the establishment of the visible form of community life according

to the institute, and to protect domestic order.
Therefore is their observance exacted from
every one in particular and from all together:
for it is by them that all must acquire a common physiognomy and appear as the members
of the same body; it is by them that they recognize one another as brethren, and that a same
family likeness shows them to be all the children of a same mother.

But, besides this general fruit, already so
fitted to excite every one to a diligent observance of the common rules, they still contain
for him the fruit of personal sanctity, which
assuredly deserves all his efforts. "My great
mortification is life in common," said a perfect
religious, Blessed John Berchmans; and he
thus pointed out one of the most fruitful sources
of religious perfection, since it ceaselessly
flows by a multitude of streams, and since the
keeping of the rules is truly, as the Prophet
tells us, "the legitimate and perpetual sacrifice of every day." (1)

VI. *The exercise of the virtues according to the
Rules.* The Christian and religious virtues are
common to all Christians and all religious;
but the acts of these virtues must often differ
according to the diversity of vocations, and it
is most important, for the legitimate exercise
of virtue, that attention should be paid to this
difference, even when wishing to imitate the
saints; otherwise illusions would be most easy;

(1) Sacrificium Domino legitimum, juge atque perpe-
tuum. Ezech. xlvi.

so that what is praiseworthy in one would become reprehensible in another. Thus, for example, mortification, zeal, charity to the neighbor, silence and the other virtues are to be practiced differently according to institutes and situations. This is why St. Anthony insisted upon the virtue of *discretion* as upon that whose function it is to regulate all the others. But how often would not our private discretion be at fault if reduced to its own lights? But this is the great advantage that the religious draws from his rules. they furnish him a sure direction as to the exercise of the virtues, and teach him how to practice them according to God's will and good pleasure.

VII. This might seem the proper place to examine the obligation of tending towards perfection by the practice of the rules; but this point is sufficiently explained by "The Catechism of the Vows," (1) and can be found more amply treated in Rodriguez, (2) and F. Saint-Jure. (3)

ARTICLE V.

THE VOWS OF RELIGION ARE MADE ACCORDING TO THE RULE OR THE CONSTITUTIONS: DIVERS DEGREES OF RELIGIOUS PERFECTION.

The vows of religion are made according to the special and proper rule of each institute:

(1) Part 2d, chap. III, art. 2.
(2) Christian Perfection, part 1st, 1st treatise, ch. 6.
(3) The Religious Man, book I, ch. 3.

that is to say, that he who makes them should understand them and bind himself to observe them according to the sense given them by the constitutions of the religious body to which he is admitted.

From this is evident the obligation devolving on superiors of thoroughly instructing novices on this point, and of assuring themselves that all the religious under them always retain an exact understanding of it.

But there is another consequence which affects the present matter, it is that the more or less perfect manner in which the rule intends the three vows of religion to be practiced, gives rise to different degrees of religious perfection itself.

There is doubtless, *a perfection common* to all institutes and it is found in the common profession of the evangelical counsels, by the three essential vows of religion.

But there is also *a perfection special* to every institute, which is proposed in common to all the members belonging thereto. This perfection depends upon the manner in which the rule requires the three evangelical counsels to be observed, it is more or less elevated according as the practice of the counsels imposed by the vows and rules is more or less perfect.

There is, finally, *a personal perfection* which becomes peculiar to every religious according as he applies himself effectually to draw it from his own institute; and this individual perfection still presents a multitude of divers degrees, depending both on the interior principle of grace and on the co-operation of every one with it.

This personal perfection is the most worthy of consideration : first, because at bottom it is the very one that gives to the religious his true merit before God ; and also, because whilst calling such a person to an institute less perfect in itself, God may still destine him to a greater interior perfection, and by means of special graces raise him, if he be faithful, to a higher degree of sanctity.

Personal perfection has its growths and so to say its ages. For the perfection of the novice is one thing, that of the religious who advances another, and still another that of the consummate religious. "Perfection is exacted from all," says St. Bernard, (1) "but not a uniform perfection. If you begin, begin perfectly ; if you are in way of progress be so perfectly, and if you have already attained some kind of perfection, measure yourself, and say with the Apostle : 'No, I have not yet reached the goal, but pursuing my course in the desire and hope of attaining it, forgetting the things that are behind, I stretch myself forward to those that are before.' " Charity causes those

(1) Ab omnibus perfectio exigitur, licet non uniformis: si incipis, perfecte incipe; si jam in profectu es, hoc ipsum perfecte age; sin autem aliquid perfectionis attigisti, teipsum in teipso metire et die cum Apostolo: non quod jam apprehenderim aut perfectus sim, sequor autem si quo modocomprehendam, quæ retro sunt obliviscens, ad ea vero quæ sunt priora extendens meipsum. De vita solitar.

who are really more advanced to redouble their ardor and hasten their speed. Charity is like the law of gravity of bodies which accelerates their movement and increases their swiftness the nearer they approach the centre of gravitation.

ARTICLE VI.

COMPARISON OF THE DIFFERENT STATES IN THE CHURCH CONSIDERED IN REFERENCE TO PERFECTION.

It seems useful to present this comparison on ending the chapter on *the State of Perfection*, it is perfectly elucidated by the Angelical Doctor. (1)

§ I.

The royal prophet compares the spouse, holy church, to a queen whose vesture is gold surrounded by a variety of colors. (2) This robe of gold is charity, and the variety of colors that enhance its splendor is the diversity of *states*, *offices* and *degrees* in the church.

The *states* in which the members of the church are placed are distinguished according as the persons in them are bound to evangelical perfection in a more or less fixed manner. (3)

The distinction among *offices* or *functions* is drawn from the fact that such or such a class of persons is deputed in the church to accom-

(1) 2a, 2æ, q. 183, a. 2, et q. 184, a. 7 et 8.

(2) Astitit regina a dextris tuis in vestitu deaurato, circumdata varietate. Psalm xliv.

(3) See above—Ch. II, art. 2, sec. 1.

plish acts that are necessary to it, as for example, acts of ecclesiastical ministry.

Finally, the *degrees* are different in the same state or office, according as some are more or less elevated than others, either by reason of their authority or their dignity and their right to honor.

Bishops have the supreme rank, not only according to degree and office, but also as to perfection of state: for they are fixed in a position which irrevocably engages them in the keeping and the care of the flock of Jesus Christ, and this state is the state of perfection, even superior to the religious state. The reason is this, that in order to lead others to perfection, it is necessary to be already perfect oneself, whilst to be lead thither, the will to tending thereunto is all that is necessary: so that the bishop is in the *state of acquired perfection,* and the religious only in the *state of perfection to be acquired.* Therefore did Our Lord say to St. Peter before confiding to him His sheep; "Simon, Son of John, lovest thou Me?" And it is only after a threefold affirmative answer that He added: "Feed my lambs, feed my sheep:" (1) but to the religious He is satisfied with saying: "If thou wilt be perfect, go sell what thou hast . . . . and come follow me." (2)

And why does not a bishop vow poverty and obedience like the religious? Because he is supposed no longer to need these two means

---

(1) John, xxi, 15, 16, 17.   (2) Matth. xix, 21.

which serve to acquire perfection, since he must already possess it through charity; and again, because once called to the episcopate, the practice of those vows is no longer compatible with his office and his rank; for he is in a post in which he must command rather than obey; and he must have wherewith to provide for even the temporal needs of the people of his diocese. But the perfection of his state imposes a more stringent obligation upon him than upon any other, of despoiling himself on occasions of pressing need for the relief of his flock.

The *state* of simple priest is not, in itself, *a state of perfection;* for the vow of continence does not give him all that is necessary to be in this state, although it does raise him above the common state; and besides, he is not as the bishop essentially and irrevocably bound to the guidance of the flock of Jesus Christ. Therefore his state is called *the state of secular priest*, which compared with that of the religious is as a lesser sacrifice compared with the holocaust.

In relation to *order*, the priest whatever be his state, secular or regular, is deputed by the Church to perform most holy actions, especially in the adorable mysteries of the Eucharist. Thence his obligation to a sanctity or interior perfection which should surpass even that which God demands from the lay religious; so that if the priest acts contrary to sanctity, he is more reprehensible than the simple religious, although the latter, on his side, finds in his state both means of sanctification and also obligations which the secular priest has not.

On account of this greater sanctity exacted of the priest, St. Jerome said to the lay religious of his time (and most of them were so then): "Live in the monastery so as to merit holy orders." (1) And in fact, how many religious in the state of perfection have found means of becoming more worthy of the priesthood! But having become regular priests, surely they lost none of the advantages given by their state, to be priests ever more perfect and more holy.

The *degree* or the post wherein a priest is placed in the Church, whether he be secular or regular, for instance, administering a parish, gives him certain powers not possessed by a simple regular priest; but this degree changes nothing in his state in reference to perfection; it only creates obligations and difficulties for him that require a more solid virtue and a greater interior sanctity. We have already seen as to the difficulties met by man in the performance of his duties, that a distinction must be made between the difficulties that diminish the merit and those that increase it. (2)

§ II.

We add here an incidental question that is connected with the preceding, and that will

(1) Sic vive in monasterio ut clericus esse merearis.
(1) See above—Ch. II, art. 2, sec. 2.

be somewhat interesting to examine and solve: *Do the regulars belong to the hierarchy?* I answer that two kinds of hierarchy are to be distinguished in Holy Church: the first is *the hierarchy of divine law*, namely that established by Jesus Christ Himself; and the second is *the hierarchy of ecclesiastical law*, that is which has been added to the first by the Church.

The hierarchy of divine law is composed of the Bishops, priests and other inferior ministers: this is a point of Catholic faith defined by the Council of Trent. (1) It is evident that no difference is to be made in this hierarchy between a regular and a secular cleric.

The hierarchy of ecclesiastical law is divided into two bodies: one is *the general and principal hierarchy*, that presides over the government of the *universal* Church; the other is *the special hierarchy af the regulars*.

The general and *principal* hierarchy was established to facilitate the good administration of the whole Christian people. Thence in the episcopal order the degrees of patriarch, primate, metropolitan, and in the second order, those of archpriests, archdeacons, parish priests, curates, etc. These degrees have varied in the Church according to times, places and needs. The regulars are not excluded by their state from this general hierarchy; there have even been epochs during which it contained more regulars than seculars.

(1) Sess. 23d, can. 6.

The special hierarchy of the regulars is only secondary and essentially dependent on the heads of the first, notably on its supreme *Hierarch*, the Roman Pontiff, Vicar of Jesus Christ. But it is a true hierarchy, constituted with its proper degrees; it comprises abbots and other regular prelates of divers names, general, provincial and local superiors; and this hierarchy, as well as the other, reascends to the head of the Church who is strictly and peculiarly the Supreme Prelate of all regulars.

The regular clergy comes after the secular clergy when it is question of the *precedence of honor*, unless they belong also to the principal hierarchy. Besides the humility of which they make profession by state, would be sufficient to impose this upon them as a duty.

As to *jurisdiction*, not only regular but also ecclesiastical in the exterior forum, regular prelates, in exempted orders, possess it over their inferiors; whilst the sacerdotal functions of pastors do not give it to them over their parishes.

Finally as to *interior jurisdiction* over the faithful in the sacrament of penance, secular priests, whoever they may be, possess it only in so far as it is communicated to them by the bishop in his diocese, either by ordinary commission in confiding to them a parish, or by extraordinary commissions in giving them the powers of hearing confessions. Exempted regular priests, although receiving this jurisdic-

tion from the Pope through their superiors,
nevertheless may not exercise it validly in any
diocese except with the approbation of the
Ordinary as was regulated by the Council of
Trent.

§ III.

A few words remain to be said about the
works of the regular clergy in the Church.
Outside of the general hierarchy this clergy is
divided into two classes of priests. Some are
solely employed, at least ordinarily, in the
clerical functions directly relating to the divine worship: such are certain orders of regular canons, and the contemplative religious
orders of the Benedictines, Carthusians, Cis-
tercians, etc. Others belong to institutes having also as an end to labor for the salvation of
souls, as the *Mendicant* orders, and those properly called *orders of regular clerics*. All these
institutes provide the ministers of the Church
charged with the ordinary care of the faithful,
with co-operators and auxiliaries: this is the
providential destination of that portion of the
regular clergy; and the Sovereign Pontiff especially looks upon it and employs it as his force
of reserves, for the greater good of the entire
Church. Every one has heard of the vision
of Innocent III (1) in which St. Francis, at
the time he was petitioning for the approbation of his Order, was shown to him supporting the Lateran Church which seemed about

(1) **Brev. Rom.**, 4th October.

to tumble into ruins. Likewise in the prayer of St. Ignatius' office, the Church has all her priests to say: "O God, Who through the blessed Ignatius hast strengthened the militant Church with a new enlistment;" (1) whence we see that the regular clergy, although only an auxiliary in the sacred hierarchy, presents it, however, with an ordinary and constant help that is furnished by God to His Church, and that the Church itself desires to see put to use for its own greater advantage and for that of its children.

CHAPTER III.

THE DIFFERENT KINDS OF VOWS OF RELIGION.

In order to throw more light on this matter we will again consider some things that lie back of it.

ARTICLE I.

OF THE RELIGIOUS STATE IN GENERAL AND OF INSTITUTES IN PARTICULAR.

According to Suarez, there are several notable differences to be pointed out between the religious state and religious institutes.

I. *The religious state*, if considered as to its substance, was instituted by Jesus Christ Himself, so that it may be said to be *of divine law*,

---

(1) Deus, qui ad majorem tui nominis gloriam propagandam novo per beatum Ignatium subsidio militantem Ecclesiam roborasti. . . . .

and that the Church has not power of abro-
gating it. This, says Suarez, is a sentiment
common to all Catholics who think correctly.
St. Francis de Sales adds, that the religious
state belongs to the *note of sanctity* of the Church,
because this character is to be manifested exteriorly by the exercise of the evangelical virtues in their highest degree: which requires
the existence of the state of perfection.

II. But *the common or cenobitical life* led in
the regular institutes is not essential to the
religious state. A person may apply himself
to perfection in private life, and if bound in a
fixed and permanent manner to the practice of
the three evangelical counsels, he may be considered as a religious. Such were the ancient
ascetics, the anchorites and the virgins and
the widows consecrated to God. However, as
we have already remarked, private life can
only with great difficulty give the means of
practicing religious poverty and obedience as
completely as can be done in community.
Whence it is that the religious state is divided
into the *complete* and the *incomplete* state of perfection.

According to the actual law of the Church,
its express approbation is rigorously needed
to constitute a true state of religion. There
is no doubt that at least the practical approbation of the Church was always necessary for
real admission into that state and in order
that he who professed it should truly be a
religious; for the religious profession consists

in a special gift of his person made to God by
the Christian, and in order to be valid this
donation must be accepted; now, God does
not accept it immediately by Himself, but
through His Church which holds towards us
His place on earth.

Nevertheless it must be said that, in the first
centuries of Christianity, this practical approbation of the Church was very often tacit and
not expressed. As to the approbation of the
Holy See it was only from the Lateran Council,
under Innocent III and from that of Lyons
under Gregory X that it was required even
for the religious orders properly so-called.

III. Formerly, stability in such an institute
or under such a rule was not exacted for the religious profession. Until the eleventh century,
there was but one monastic order, or rather
there was none, although there were several
rules, but they were variable at the will of
the superiors. To speak exactly, the religious
state alone existed, without those precise differences which now constitute the diversity of
institutes. There was then no obligation to
attach oneself to a special community; it was
sufficient to manifest by some outward sign
that one was altogether consecrated to God,
and one thus belonged to the religious state,
with the obligation of persevering therein, but
without being bound to belong to a particular
monastery or to be subject to any one rule, unless by some formal engagement. It was St.
Benedict who, to put an end to the frequent

and prejudicial passages from one monastery to another, established the celebrated sanction of *stability*, which his religious had to promise: a most salutary institution which soon becoming a rule universally consecrated by the authority of the Church, also became the principle of the diversity of institutes.

ARTICLE II.

THE VARIETY OF RELIGIOUS INSTITUTES.

SECTION I.—*Causes and Ends of this Diversity.*

I. The diversity of religious institutes in the Church is not the effect of chance nor the fruit of the caprice of men. It has its first cause in the conduct of Divine Providence and in the interior operations of the Holy Ghost in the depths of souls.

In destining to each man his place upon earth, God gave him qualities, aptitudes and tastes suitable to this destination: so that the diversity met with in characters, talents, inclinations and even corporal strength and needs, contributes to determinate the different choices which fix some in one position of life, and others in another, as much for the common good of society as for the direction of every one towards the final end of his creation, which is, eternal salvation. Now, with greater reason is this providential disposition of God shown in those whom He destines by a more special vocation to the state of evangelical perfection. It is morally impossible that all aptitudes and all propensities should accommodate themselves to a single manner of living in that state.

One will feel more facility and attraction for a life of contemplation, mortification and silence; another will find the occupations of an active life more suited to his nature, tastes and impulses of grace; finally, a third will see in the gifts received by him in a divided manner, indications of a vocation to a life of mixed contemplation and action; and thus all will have the means of tending to perfection by the exercise of charity towards God and the neighbor, but under different forms and in divers measures.

II.—Still further, God Who always has in view the good of His Church, knows how to obtain it by this same action of His Providence and of His Holy Spirit in souls. As the needs of the faithful people are very various, one same and single institute could not embrace them all together; but Divine Goodness has provided for this by the diversity of religious bodies and destines them, every one doing its share and acting in its own way to procure for the Church some spiritual or temporal good, and to come to the help of its children in their evils of body and soul. Institutes have their vocation as well as individuals. Being members of the great body of the Church, they each receive, like the members of the human body, an end proper to themselves and a special destination, in which they are to concur to the general welfare. Some more withdraw into solitude, pray for the Church and edify it by good example; (1) others in closer communication with men, labor for the salvation of souls or give themselves up to other works of mercy.

SECTION II.—*Three Principal Kinds of Religious Institutes.*

I. It is seen from what has been said that all religious institutes can be ranged in three principal classes, according as the *contemplative*, the *active* or the *mixed life* is led therein.

To the contemplative life belong the purely *monastic orders*, because their special and direct end is to devote themselves to prayer and to the exercises of Divine worship. Therein work itself is subordinate and auxiliary to this principal end: such are the Benedictines, Carthusians, Poor Clares, Carmelites, etc.

The active life is proper to those numerous institutes which give themselves to the care of the poor or the sick, or to the rearing and education of children. We may rank in this class, the orders that devote themselves to the ransom of captives and the military orders employed in the defence of Christianity against the infidels.

The mixed life is that wherein contemplation and action are united and go, so to say, hand in hand; then the exercises of the con-

(1) Beautiful pages on this subject may be read in the Introduction of M. de Montalembert's "Monks of the West."

templative life give to the religious the lights
and the graces of which he has need for himself and his neighbor; whilst by action and
above all by the ministry of the priesthood, he
strives to communicate to others the goods
that he has received; and thus closely uniting
the work of his own perfection to that of the
sanctification of his neighbor he imitates the
life of the Apostles: who said of themselves
"But we will give ourselves continually to
prayer and to the ministry of the word."(1)
In this class may be numbered the orders of
St. Dominic, St. Francis, St. Ignatius, etc.

A serious remark to be made to the religious
who are in the active life, is this—they themselves need to borrow from the contemplative
life a suitable measure of spiritual exercises;
without which they shall be in danger, in the
midst of exterior occupations, of forgetting what
they owe to their own perfection or even to the
personal affair of their own salvation, according to the advice Our Lord gives them : "Martha,
Martha, thou art careful and art troubled
about many things. But one thing is necessary." (2)   The world which admires the Sister
of Charity and acknowledges the value of her
services, yet finds fault with her devotions.

When it reproaches her with losing the time
that she consecrates to them, it has not the
slightest suspicion that without this no Sister
of Charity would be possible; but could she

(1) Acts, vi, 4.
(2) Luke, x, 41, 42.

herself share this gross illusion or act practically as if she shared it by neglecting her spiritual exercises ?

II.—If it is wished to establish a comparison among these three lives in reference to perfection, and among the institutes which exercise them, these are the principles laid down by St. Thomas : (1)

The difference between one order and another is *principally* considered in the end proper to each, and *secondarily* according to the means employed to obtain it. That one is therefore *absolutely* better which proposes to itself a better end. Therefore an order living the contemplative life is *in itself* better than that exercising the active life; according to what Our Lord said to Martha, sister of Mary : "Mary hath chosen the better part:" for, according to the Fathers, these two sisters are the figures of the two lives ; Martha representing the active life in the service of the Divine Master, and Mary serving as a figure of the contemplative life.

It may be remarked here that it is not according to these principles that the spirit of the world judges religious institutes, and that consequently it deceives itself in its appreciations.

There are however certain works of the active life that flow from the plenitude of contemplation, as preaching and the care of the sanctification of souls ; and this is better than

(1) 2a, 2æ, q. 188, a. 6.

simple contemplation: for it is more perfect to communicate to others the truths which have been contemplated by one's self than to confine one's self to contemplating them alone, as it is better to illuminate than merely to shine. This is why institutes wherein the labor for one's own perfection is joined to that for the sanctification of the neighbor, occupy the first rank of excellence among others; this is, in fact, the life led by the apostles, after the great model of all perfection, Jesus Christ, Himself.

If the end of several institutes is equally good and perfect, the pre-eminence is then judged secondarily by the means used for obtaining that end. And as the means are established not for themselves, but for the end, it follows that not the more rigid observances are to be judged the better, but those that are better proportioned to the end of the institute.

ARTICLE III.

SOLEMN, SIMPLE, PERPETUAL AND TEMPORARY VOWS OF RELIGION.

I.—What is exactly meant by solemn or simple vows is explained by "The Catechism of the Vows." (1)

It likewise pointed out that solemn vows exist only in religious orders properly so-called; and this is the essential difference distinguishing these orders from simple religious congre-

(1) Part 1st, ch. 3.

gations. It must be added that all the members of a religious order properly so-called do not always make solemn profession, but that there are some in which many are at least at first, allowed to make only simple vows; and that these vows, although simple, render the persons who utter them religious, in the strict sense of the word, as has been declared by Pope Gregory XIII of the simple vows pronounced by the scholastics of the Society of Jesus.

Pope Pius IX, in an extraordinary congregation, convoked March 19th, 1857, *on the state of regulars*, decreed for all religious orders in which solemn profession of the vows was made at the end of only one year, that thenceforth it would be permitted to pronounce only the simple vows of religion after this single year of novitiate, and that a further trial during three more years would be required to be admitted to the solemn profession of these same vows.

According to a declaration of the Holy See, (1) the simple vows of which we have just spoken, can be annulled by the superior of the Order, in case and by the very fact of the *legitimate dismissal* of the subject. Otherwise recourse must be had to the Sovereign Pontiff for a dispensation.

II.—The "Catechism" in reference to the merit of *perpetual* or *temporary* vows, offers two

(1) Analecta Juris Pontificii, 1860.

propositions which in their brevity require explanation. (1)

1st. It says that "an inferior vocation can have its compensations:" in order that this proposition should be true it must have the condition understood that God is the author of this vocation; for if alleged against God's call, it would cease to be exact and true. Nevertheless, when a person is no longer free to repair the wrong, it may be a consolation and should serve as a spur to good will.

2ndly. It also says: "To engage one's self but for a time presents the occasion of reiterating one's sacrifice with full liberty." This proposition would be completely false if it be meant for a person limiting himself to the temporary vow through a want of generosity, when comparing him with another person who has had · the courage to give himself to God for all time, and who would be ready to do so again every day of his life, and who, after all, remains in full possession of his interior liberty. Even as to his exterior liberty, there may have been more merit, also, by forestalling his own instability by the bond of the perpetual vow.

III. Three principal conditions are necessary to render valid the admission to the vows of religion : first, it must be made by competent superiors according to the constitutions: second, the one admitted to the vows must have reached the age fixed by the Church and by the approved institute; third, the admis-

(1) Part 1st, ch. 3.

sion to the vows must have been preceded by a novitiate at the very least of one year; several institutes add the obligation of a second year and sometimes more.

Other conditions may also exist necessary for the validity of the vows, according to the constitutions of the divers orders or congregations.

IV. The novitiate positively begins for the candidate only after his admission by the competent superior and even only from the moment of his real entrance into probation.

Its duration must be for a full and entire year, and cannot be abridged by a single day or even less; so that the vows would be null if pronounced before the complete expiration of the year, even were it leap year. Whence is seen how great should be the exactitude to note down the day of the positive entrance to the novitiate. There are institutes in which it is established by rule that should the vows perchance be null through this defect or that of want of age, they become valid at the first public renovation of them afterwards made.

The duration of the novitiate must be continuous, so that there shall be for the novice no interruption in it, at least none moral. A sickness which should prevent him from taking part in the exercises proper to the novitiate, and even *a short absence for a legitimate reason*, would not break the sufficient continuity. But should the novice be sent away or forsake his vocation himself, there would then be a moral interruption: consequently, in case of return, he would be obliged to begin over his entire novitiate.

———

ARTICLE IV.

OF THE DESIRE A RELIGIOUS MAY HAVE TO PASS TO ANOTHER INSTITUTE.

I. This is St. Thomas' doctrine upon this question considered in a general way. (1)

It must be said that it is no praiseworthy thing to pass from one institute to another, unless through necessity or for some great utility: either because those from whom separation is made are scandalized, or because, all things being equal, one does better in an order wherein one has grown accustomed to serve God, than in another.

It may, nevertheless, be laudable to pass to another order for one of these three reasons: first, the love and desire inspired by God for a more perfect institute. It must be remarked that this superiority in the perfection of one institute over another is to be judged not solely by the austerity of the observance of the rules, but principally by the end that the order proposes to itself, and secondarily by the wise proportion of the means to the end of the institute, as has been set forth above. (2)

The second reason might be the decay of the order in which one is. If then that order

(1) 2a, 2æ, q. 189, a. 8.
(2) Chap. III, art. II, sec. II, § II.

should have wandered from the perfection of its institute, it would be praiseworthy to pass even to a less strict order in which the rule would be better observed.

The third reason would be the inability of a religious to observe a rule too rigid for him, whilst he could follow another which would be less severe.

But it must be observed, that in the first case, the religious must ask, through humility, the permission, which still may not be refused him, provided he be certain that the order into which he wishes to pass is of a more strict observance. If there be any doubt upon this point, he is to take the advice of the superior, as prescribed by Canon law. The second case also requires that the religious should consult the superior. But in the third case a dispensation is necessary.

II. This is exactly the doctrine of the Church as to the passage of a religious from one institute to another; we shall add some short explanations. 1st. It is therefore, generally speaking, permitted to a religious who has made the vows according to one rule to pass to a more perfect institute. Which arises, as we have already said, (1) from the right that every one retains, after making a vow of commuting it to a better one. Moreover, although God may have been really the author of the first vocation, it is evident that He ever remains the Master of His creature; and that,

(1) Chap. I, art. III.

besides, even if He has fixed it at a post, He without contradicting Himself, call it later to a higher one. We find examples of this in many Saints, such as St. Anthony of Padua, etc.

2ndly. We said, *generally speaking*, because there are orders and even simple religious congregations from which a passage to another institute, has been, for just motives, forbidden by the Holy See, at least without the formal sanction of superiors.

3dly. It is to be remarked, that, in order to be legitimate, this desire of passing to another institute, even though it be more perfect, must come from God, and it is a duty for him who feels it to assure himself of this; for when a person is already settled according to the Divine Will, nothing is more dangerous than the temptation presented by the enemy of salvation on this point to human inconstancy.

"For those who desire what is good," says St. Ignatius, the devil applies himself above all to lead astray their good will; he feigns that he wishes nothing but to favor this good will, and he proposes to it what is apparently and fictitiously better in order to bring a soul to his perverse ends. (1)

A case of this nature exacts a very special examination; because manifest proofs in order to be convinced of a new call for God, more are required than even for the first vocation. This person, during his whole novitiate, had no doubt contrary to the vocation he was en-

(1) Spirit. Exer., Rules on the discernment of spirits.

tering; how could he now imagine that God demands of him so important a change? This, in our view, is an ordinary means of judging the question, and a superabundant reason for rejecting, at the very first, such thoughts as dangerous suggestions. A case deserving of some examination, might perhaps be that of a person who then knew no other institute than the one that he entered, or again that wherein, some indication has subsequently become apparent of which account should have been taken.

4thly. As to the motive of changing that is drawn from the decay of a congregation, it would certainly be legitimate, as St. Thomas declares, if it unfortunately had foundation or above all if there resulted therefrom a peril to the salvation of the religious. But it must be said that every relaxation that a person may imagine that he sees is not sufficient to authorize so grave a determination. A dissatisfied or fretful spirit often creates what does not exist, or exaggerates what does; and it does not know how to make allowances for human infirmity, that is found wherever there are men. The criticism is unjust when it casts upon the whole institute the blame deserved by some individuals. Finally, even if the religious body of which one is member be not all that it should be, it may happen that God requires what holy religious have done in like cases : namely, that one should show love of one's order and brethren, by applying one's self to remedy the evil according to the grace that one has received, were it only by the humble protestation of good example.

Therefore, the desire of leaving one's institute and passing to another is rarely praiseworthy and is seldom the effect of an impulse of grace. Esteem and love of one's vocation, with an inviolable attachment to the holy state in which one has been consecrated to the Lord, is as we are going now to show, the common order and in general the great duty of religious.

ARTICLE V.

OF ESTEEM AND LOVE OF ONE'S OWN VOCATION.

I —The Apostle St. Paul has beautiful words on this subject: "See your vocation, brethren, he says, (1) "fix your eyes ceaselessly upon it: upon yours and not on that of others. Let each remain in the vocation to which he has been called. (2) ... I beseech you that you walk worthy of the vocation in which you are called." (3)

There are some vocations higher than others, there are institutes proposing to their members a perfection superior to that of some other institute; this is an indisputable principle, as seen in the preceding article. But a no less certain principle and one more practical in its applications, is that there is a distinction to be made between two sorts of goods or perfec-

(1) I Cor. i, 26.   (2) I Cor. i.   (3) Ephes. iv, 1.

tions: there is the good that draws its goodness from the *object*, and the good that owes its goodness to the *subject*. A purely objective better and one considered apart from the agent, is only an abstraction, a speculation of the mind without reality; the real better, more agreeable to God, more meritorious for man, is the subjective or personal better; and this better depends upon two things which must be united: on one hand upon God's vocation and grace, on the other upon our faithful correspondence with this vocation and grace; in a word this better consists in the will of God executed in every point; and it is found only therein. You aspire after something better which the Lord does not ask of you, and you neglect the good that He assigns to you! Know that instead of a real and personal better you shall find only deception and mistake.

But know also that when God does invite you to ascend higher, to refuse and obstinately remain lower, under pretence that this is enough for your ambition, and that besides you know how to tend therein to what is better for you personally, is a want of generosity, an infidelity, and an error full of perils.

II. This is the sovereign rule in the service of God, our supreme and universal Lord. "To serve God," says St. Ignatius, with an admirable and energetic clearness of expression, "is to place ourselves at His disposition, that He Himself may use us according to the whole

extent of His Will and Good Pleasure;''(1) and
the saint gives the comparison of the *tool*,
which never resists the workman whatever use
he may make of it. Nothing is more practical
than this luminous maxim, as much so for entering a state of life as for remaining therein,
when it has been taken according to God, as
much so for the order to be chosen, the office, the
time and the place, as for every one of our
actions.

Since we refer here to the first principle of
every vocation, let us still add one remark:
Certain persons are often heard to ask themselves in relation to the choice they have to
make of a state of life: "In which shall I do
the most good?" The question is badly put,
they should say: "In which state does God
wish me to do good and for what kind of good
does He wish to make use of me?" For I am to
attach and apply myself to the good that God
wills of me, even were it less than the one I
imagine. It is, in fact, evident that this is
the essential condition of a servant towards his
Master, and the disposition in which he should
ever be. But, moreover, it is easily seen that
these persons when speaking of the greater
good they are to do in a state of life, think ordinarily only of the good that they are to do
to others; and they forget, by a manifest illusion, that the first good to be thought of is
their own good, good to their soul; and most
certainly we can hope to do that good only

(1) Exerc. Spir., Prælud. ad consider. Stat.

there where God promises us His help by the vocation that He Himself gives us.

III.—This principle once laid down, the consequences are easily drawn.

1st. The finest vocation for me, is that that comes to me really from God. The gift which merits my preference is that which He has deigned to give me. The situation wherein I can do the most good, and, before all else, work out the good of my own sanctification is that that He has judged well to assign to me.

2nd. I must doubtless, esteem every institute raised by the Spirit of God and approved by His Church; but I am to love my own institute most: as a child loves his mother above every other person, even though she be less rich or less beautiful.

3rdly. Piety, justice and charity oblige me to recognize and praise in all religious bodies the manifold grace of the Holy Ghost, Who by this marvellous variety provides for all the needs of bodies and souls; but it is also my duty, to recognize with a still more loving heart the special grace of my vocation and all the benefits of which it is the source for me.

4thly. One of the most important obligations of every religious is to nourish the love and esteem of his vocation. He who allows these two great things to be weakened in him, shows that he himself is becoming relaxed in the fidelity that he owes to God, and, instead of accusing his institute, he would be nearer the

truth if he accused himself, in order to recall
himself efficaciously to exactitude and fervor.

CHAPTER IV.

ON THE VIRTUES WHICH ARE THE OBJECT OF THE THREE VOWS OF RELIGION.

ARTICLE I.

DIFFERENCES EXISTING BETWEEN THE VOW AND THE VIRTUE.

"The Catechism of the Vows" points out
four differences between the vow and the virtue, and gives of every one of them a sufficient
explanation. (1)   But as it does no more than
indicate certain practical lessons flowing therefrom, we shall do well to insist thereon a little
more strongly in order that the diligence of
persons consecrated to God may be excited by
their consideration.

I.—The first difference shows in the vow a
means relative to the virtue: whence is apparent the inconsistency of those relaxed religious,
who after making the vow, neglect the virtue.

The better to make them feel this fatal inconsistency they should be confronted with the
fervent religious that have been given by the
same vocation; the sight of these domestic
examples will be a powerful spur to excite
them; for it is only by resembling them that

(1) Part 1st, chap. IV.

they can legitimately glory in having them as brethren.

Their ardor may likewise be re-awakened by showing them the saints who even out of the cloister have ascended so high in the perfection of the virtues, although these were not bound to the Lord by vows, as they are. What do I say? Even the thought of so many generous souls which the Church can ever present to them from the midst of the world, will be for them a subject of salutary confusion. Ah! if God had granted to these fervent Christians a vocation such as theirs, with all the means of sanctification that it contains, what would not have been their correspondence and their fidelity?

These are reflections that it would be scarcely possible to make seriously without being touched; and thus shall a religious turn away the danger that threatens him in the midst of his abundance, that of growing accustomed to the gifts of God even so far as to cease esteeming them, according to St. Augustine's expression (1) and thereby soon reaching the terrible evil of tepidity and abuse.

II.—The second difference between the vow and the virtue is that the vow cannot properly extend beyond what it imposes under pain of sin, whilst the virtue can rise to a perfection ever higher and higher.

From this again a great consequence is to be drawn, namely, that it is by zeal in increasing

(1) Assiduitate vilnerunt.

in virtue from day to day that one becomes a
good religious. This truth will be better understood by means of a comparison in the commandments of God we distinguish the part
called *negative* which always obliges under pain
of sin, and the part called *positive* which, without always binding the conscience, guides man
to an ever more perfect observance of the commandment. For instance, the first three precepts of the decalogue in their negative part,
forbid under pain of divine offence everything
that is contrary to the worship due to God; but
they go far higher in their positive part, since
they embrace all the degrees of perfection by
which the true servant of God should strive to
exercise acts therein: and the same may be
said of the other commandments as to the matter
that is peculiar to them. Now, vows are obligations that a man imposes upon himself by
the promise that he makes to God, and they
become thus a kind of personal precept wherein
a negative and a positive part may be distinguished: the first is the proper matter of the
vow obliging under pain of sin; the second is
the matter of the virtue wherein the true religious should tend to an ever increasing perfection.

The religious found in communities can be
divided into three divers classes: the *mediocre
religious*, the *good religious*, the *holy religious;*
for we put aside a fourth class, the *bad religious*, since they are in fact no religious, or
only to their condemnation.

To these three classes may be applied what St. Ignatius says of the three sorts of persons who give themselves to the spiritual exercise of a retreat: "Some *walk* at their ease and without going out of the narrow space they have marked for themselves; others *take the pace of a traveller* who walks more briskly and does not limit the space he is to traverse until he has reached the end of his journey; the third do more still, *they choose a racing speed*, because they wish to go farther and arrive sooner. (1)

Thus the mediocre religious is he who proceeds slowly, satisfied to walk at his ease within certain limits wherein he goes to and fro. In him the spirit of faith and the spirit of sacrifice are weak and often wanting; his intention frequently lacks uprightness and purity, he observes his rules provided they do not constrain him too much; he does not act against virtue when what it requires is easy; but in difficulties he is often found in fault.

The good religious is he who in his career has taken the quick and resolute step of a traveller: for he seriously means to attain his end. Doubtless he is not impeccable; but his soul has elasticity; he has the true devotion spoken of by St. Thomas, that is, promptitude of will to devote himself to the things that belong to the service of God. Therefore, not only does he dread as a misfortune every sin and every violation of his vows, however slight;

(1) Spirit. Exerc., 1st Annot.

but also he habitually acts according to the
requirements of virtue, and if he sometimes
stumbles in a difficulty it is only through surprise or a momentary weakness, from which he
rises without delay.

And what is to be said of the holy religious?
He runs, and would like to fly in his career, (1)
and he repeats after the Apostle: "Not as
though I had already attained or were already
perfect, but I follow after, if I may by any means
apprehend . . . forgetting the things that are
behind and stretching forth myself to those
that are before." (2)   Nevertheless believe not
that he is without temptations, without difficulties, without failings, without falls and even
without sins.   No, this perfect delivery belongs
not to the saints of this world; and know well
that the trials God sends them are even greater
than yours, because He proportions them to
their virtue.   But what does belong to the
holy religious is the single will, and consequently strong and constant, the will to go
to God by disengaging himself from everything else, the will to profit by all things, even
by his defects and faults in order the better to
rise towards the one object of his love.   And
his great means of attaining that end are his
vows and his rules, together with abnegation
and patience, the spirit of faith, confidence and
humility.

(1) Who will give me wings like a dove and I will fly?
Psalm liv, 7. They shall take wings as eagles and they
shall fly and not weary. Isaias, xl, 31.
(2) Philippians, iii, 12, 13.

It must be said, moreover, that fervent communities are not only those in which saints only are to be found, nor those in which no defects are to be met with. Alas! it is in vain that such would be sought on earth. There are always mediocre religious in a good community; but the good form the majority. May it please Our Divine Master to keep the bad entirely away, and ever grant it also a few saints!

III. The third difference between the virtue and the vow consists in this, that the virtue is, in its turn, a means relative to the vow: so that the more diligent will a religious be in practising the virtue, so much safer shall he be as to the violation of the vow. But he must know also, that when he notably neglects the exercise of the virtue, he infallibly approaches infidelity to his vow. This pressing motive of applying himself to virtue is perfectly developed in Rodriguez "Christian Perfection." (1)

IV. The fourth difference lays down this principle, that a religious can sin against the virtue without violating his vow: whence two important truths must be gathered: first, that every failing against poverty or obedience is not necessarily a sin against these vows; secondly, that he cannot always say: "My vow is not violated, therefore there is no sin."

(1) Part III, 6th Treatise, chapters 1 and 5.

ARTICLE II.

OTHER OBLIGATIONS RESULTING FROM THE RELIGIOUS
PROFESSION, BESIDES THAT OF THE VOWS THEM-
SELVES.

The obligations of which we are about to
speak result from the *act of donation*, which
the religious by his profession, makes of his
person, to the institute in which he pronounces
his vows.

SECTION I.— *What are those Obligations.*

Every man presenting himself to become a
member of a body, and who is eventually accepted as such, binds himself and contracts obligations towards that body: obligation of stability according to the nature of the engagement taken upon himself; obligation of con-
curring with the common good and the common end; obligation of following the direction and impulse of those legitimately govern-
ing; obligation of maintaining union and con-
cord with the other members; obligation of
loving with a special affection the body and
the members of the body of which he forms a
part; obligation, finally, of overcoming the
obstacles which may oppose themselves to the
duties of his position.

All this is true of any association and in
proportion to the degree of connection established among the members; truer still of associations established by the Spirit of God for a
spiritual end and consecrated by the appro-

bation of the Church. But what binds together much more closely the members of a religious body is the sacred bond of the vows therein made.

Then every individual resembles a stone that is part of the construction of an edifice: a living stone, so incorporated into this living edifice, that did it wish of itself to change its destination, its place or its function, not only would it compromise the beauty of the edifice, but often its very solidity. A still more complete and more expressive comparison can be found in the natural family: for all that the ties of blood establish in the way of relations, rights and duties in the bosom of a family, the bond of the vows establish in the religious body, creating therein a spiritual paternity, filiation and brotherhood.

Without stopping longer at the other respects, we reach the place to insist upon two great points of the religious life: first, union and fraternal charity; second, the evangelical detachment of the religious from his relations.

SECTION II.—*The Duties of Religious Fraternity.*

1. It would be superfluous to prove that all that is said in the Gospel concerning Christian fraternity applies in a much more special manner to religious fraternity. And what is the mark by which Jesus Christ, Our Lord, wishes His own to be known? He Himself has told it—union and charity among brethren: "By this shall all men know that you

are My disciples, if you have love one for another." (1) Such also was the most striking characteristic of the primitive Church: "They had but one heart and one soul," declares Holy Writ; (2) and the Pagans, wondering at this novel spectacle, repeated with admiration: "See how they love one another!"

Soon, unfortunately, and as the number of Believers multiplied, charity grew cold in the hearts of many: that is why, even before the era of persecution had passed, the Spirit of Charity gave rise to those religious institutions in which He wished to preserve the sacred fire in its first purity; and whilst the common Christians often found it difficult to strictly observe the precept of charity, a multitude of pious asylums were destined to show it perpetually to the world in all its perfection. How many means have been brought together there to produce and maintain this divine result! To speak only of the holocaust of the vows, is it not a sacrifice, offered not only to God, but even to one's brethren in God's sight! And can it not be said to be equally full of divine and of fraternal love?

How much, therefore, should every religious apply himself to foster within himself that spirit of charity, and so to cause this queen of virtues to flourish in himself, that its perfume escaping from the heart of every indi-

(1) John, xiii, 35.
(2) The multitude of believers had but one heart and one soul. Acts.

vidual, shall spread throughout the entire community!

II. In order to help good will, we shall point out briefly, on one hand, what fraternal charity requires, and, on the other, what lessens it. What it requires above all are meek and humble hearts: from this source all the rest shall be seen to flow: disinterestedness, cordiality, reciprocal esteem and confidence, delicate attentions, the most effective eagerness in rendering service, and, when needed, endurance of defects and a prompt and complete forgetting of mutual wrongs.

What lessens charity and union among brethren before all other causes is egotism with its icy distinction of *mine* and *thine*, as says St. Chrysostom; (1) and, to go into details, it is pretensions and haughtiness; jealousies, impatience, rudeness and sharp words, indelicacies and familiarity or susceptibilities, poutings and rancor, antipathies and coldness or preferences and exclusive friendships: it is the spirit of curiosity and affected wit, suspicions, distrust and indiscreet reports; finally, an inclination to criticism, to disputes, to singularity of ideas, to raillery and to jokes at the expense of the brethren.

This is a double enumeration of things which can, on account of our defective nature, give a very meritorious exercise to fraternal charity every day and almost every hour. Motives of encouragement to this incessant struggle are

(1) Meum et tuum, frigidum illud verbum.

abundant, but it will be sufficient to recall the words of the great Apostle: "For he that loveth his neighbor hath fulfilled the law." (1)

III. Fraternal charity is clearly connected with *edification* and *mutual regards*.

1st. A religious truly loving his brethren will prove it especially by leading them on to good by the examples of his regularity, and will not allow himself anything which might disedify them. It is already an evil to commit faults oneself, and the least of them, when deliberate, harms a religious much; but the evil is much greater when he causes his brethren to commit them and thus places them on an incline which may become dangerous for them and lead them further than he thinks. Ah! shall not every one of us have a sufficient account to render to the sovereign Judge? Do we wish to add to it the failings to which our words and actions will have drawn others? A religious should conceive the greatest aversion for anything, which, in him, would be of a nature to disedify his brethren: such was the sentiment experienced by St. Paul, and in what energetic terms did he not express it! (2)

2dly. As to *mutual attentions* due to one another in religion, the same Apostle spoke thus

(1) Romans, xiii.
(2) But take heed lest perhaps this your liberty become a stumbling-block to the weak. . . . . Now when you sin thus against the brethren and wound their weak conscience, you sin against Christ. Wherefore if meat scandalize my brother, I will never eat flesh, lest I should scandalize my brother. I Cor. viii, 9, 12, 13.

to the first Christians; "Loving one another
with the charity of brotherhood, with honor
preventing one another; let each treat his
brother as his superior." (1) These beautiful
words express perfectly the duties of religious
fraternity. Among brethren are needed love,
cordiality and a certain freedom of intimacy
which is not to be had towards others; but to
these respect must be added among brethren
united according to God; and all owe one another esteem and honor, exacted on the one
hand by the dignity of their vocation, and on
the other by the care to recognize by faith in
every one the person and image of Jesus Christ,
Our Lord, Himself.

This fraternal respect should have two char-
acteristics: first, it ought to exist more in the
reality of deeds than in exterior forms; second,
every one should maintain therein religious
simplicity.

That it may be practical and effective, be
humble; then will your deferences be no vain
demonstrations, as are too often those of the
world. Then, according to the Gospel, you
shall always seek the last place rather than
the first, (2) what is least in the house rather
than that which is best. Multiplied applica-.
tions of this principle might be made but in a
few words I shall say all: avoid those thousand
petty artifices of self-love, always occupied with
self, always in quest of preferences and privileges.

(1) Romans, xii, 10, and Philip. ii.
(2) Sit down in the lowest place. Luke, xiv, 10.

As to the exterior expression of fraternal respect, the members of a religious community ought to strive to become perfectly polite and civil among themselves, nothing would be more unbecoming to them than clownishness and ill-breeding. But their politeness must also be modest, and the manifestations of their deference, full of simplicity: only at that price will it be charity ; and it will likewise please and edify only on that condition. Consequently religious must avoid as unworthy of their profession, far-fetched manners, affected compliments, and everything recalling the pretension and exaggeration of worldly politeness.

SECTION III.—*Of Evangelical Detachment from One's Relatives.*

Nothing is more formally expressed in the Gospel than the duty of detachment from relations for those called by God to the religious state. The Divine Master goes so far as to exact that a person called by Him should leave them for good, in order to be able to be entirely given up to His service and to the duties of that high vocation. In His design of making the religious soul His special spouse, He wishes her to apply to herself what is written of the conjugal state: "Man shall leave father and mother and shall cleave to his wife" (1); and He addresses those words of the Psalm to her: "Hearken, O daughter, and see, and incline thine ear; forget thy people and thy father's

(1) Gen. ii, 24.

house, and the King shall greatly desire thy beauty, for He is the Lord, Thy God. (1).

To show at the same time the legitimacy, the duty and the practice of this evangelical detachment, we shall specially cite the principles of St. Thomas, which are those of Holy Church and of right reason according to God.

§ I.— *What is the debt of filial piety.*

In virtue of natural right a son owes his father and mother something essential and something accidental.

A son's essential debt towards his parents, considered as such, that is, as the principles of his being and consequently his natural superiors, is *honor*, according to these words of the law: "Honor thy father and thy mother." His other duties flow from this fundamental debt, such as love, respect, obedience and service.

The accidental debt of filial piety is that which circumstances impose upon a son towards his parents. For instance, if they are poor, sick, captives, etc., he must honor them by going to their help with all means in his power. And as soon as this assistance becomes necessary and possible it admits of no excuse or dispensation.

And as parents, on their side, because they are the principal of their son's existence, have as their essential debt towards him to provide for his needs, not only for a time but during his whole life.

(1) Psalm lxiv, 11, 12.

It follows from these principles: first, that it is not allowable to a father and mother to leave their children, even to consecrate themselves to God in the religious state, before having provided for their future; 2dly, that a son may not leave his father or mother in a *serious need* of which he alone could relieve them, to follow a career that would not allow him to help them any more. If parents are in *extreme* necessity, that is, if their life be in peril, a son already a religious, is bound to succor them, even by forsaking his state, if he cannot do it otherwise. In case of a necessity serious but not extreme it is more probable, according to theologians, that he is not obliged and even that it is not allowable for him to abandon the religious state; but he is bound, under the obedience due to his superiors, to employ all the means in his power to provide for his parents' needs.

§ II.—*Are the duties of filial piety to be omitted on account of those imposed by the virtue of religion?*

Here is the Angelic Doctor's answer: (1)
Religion and filial piety are two virtues. And no virtue is contrary to another, because good can never be contrary to good. It is therefore impossible for religion and filial piety to contradict each other so that the act of the one should forbid the act of the other. In fact, the act of every virtue always has a limit set

(1) 2a, 2æ, q. 101, a. 4, and q. 189, a. 6.

by right reason ; and if it proceeded beyond this limit, it would be no longer an act of virtue but a vicious act. Thus it is of filial piety which has its limits established by reason and justice, and it is evident that these limits would be overstepped in case a son should wish to honor his father more than God. If, then, my father provokes me to evil, or wishes to withdraw me from the service that God requires of me, my duty is not to acquiesce to his will in this point; but as the Apostle says, "shall we not much more obey the Father of spirits and live ?" (1)

And this is the sense of those words of Our Lord in the gospel : "He that loveth father or mother more that me is not worthy of me."(2)

The first application of these principles is in case parents should wish to turn away their child from the service of God in things of obligation or expose him to occasions dangerous to his salvation.

But they are also applicable in case a child is really called by God to consecrate himself entirely to His worship in the religious state. In fact, St. James and St. John are praised in the Gospel for having left their father to follow Jesus Christ. Not because their father excited them to sin ; but since he could support himself, his children saw nothing to prevent them from answering the call of the Lord.

(1) Moreover we have had fathers of our flesh for our instructors and we reverenced them; shall we not much more obey the Father of spirits, and live ? Heb. xii, 9.

(2) Matt. x, 37.

When a child has attained the proper age, it is allowable for him to enter the religious state, even against his parents' will: for he then possesses his liberty in all that appertains to the disposition of his life by the choice of a state; and this liberty assuredly exists, especially when a state of life wherein God is more perfectly served, is under consideration.

Our Lord, in the Gospel (1) reproved a disciple who wished to delay answering His call, under pretext that he had first to bury his father: for, says St. Chrysostom, there were others at hand to fulfil that duty of filial piety; or, according to St. Cyril, that man asked to remain near his old father until his death, which Our Lord did not grant, as there were others whom relationship bound to take this charge.

But the objection may be made that to honor one's parents is a duty exacted by precept, whilst to enter religion is only a counsel, and consequently left to the free choice of the Christian.

I reply, first, that the precept of honoring one's parents relates not only to corporal service but also to spiritual services.

Children in the religious state can abundantly fulfil this precept by their prayers, their respect and even their good offices, as far as becomes their profession. And let it be remarked, that even those who remain in the world have not always to honor their parents

(1) Matt. viii, 21, 22.

by corporal services; but they do so in different ways according to their condition and their state.

I reply, in the second place, that a vocation to the religious state is not a thing left altogether to the Christian's liberty. Although, generally speaking, it is only a counsel, it is however a fact, that salvation is almost always dependent upon it, and were it only to assure that or to make it more easy, those whom God calls have the greatest interest not to resist His voice. And, according to the principles of the Gospel, parents cannot require their child to sacrifice the like interests to their caprice or even to their temporal advantage. Moreover, if a strong desire lead that child to the religious state, and, as often happens, the happiness even temporal of his whole life was involved, by what right could they pretend to oppose it, putting their own interest before that capital welfare of their child even in this world?

§ III.—*The love of a religious for his parents.*

The world is sometimes heard to accuse the religious state of abridging the fourth commandment of God and of smothering the love for parents in the heart of those who embrace it. Besides the answers given above, let us see how the case really stands in reference to a religious faithful to the obligations of his state.

He is, doubtless, numbered among those to whom these words are addressed: "Whosoever comes to me and hates not his father and his mother and his own life also, cannot be my disciple." Who is it that pronounced words apparently so hard? Is it not the divine author of the commandment, Himself? And this is the interpretation which, with St. Ignatius, must be given to them: "This is why the religious must despoil himself of all carnal affection towards his kindred, to change it into a spiritual affection, and love them henceforth only with that one love required by well-regulated charity: as a man, who being dead to the world and to self-love, lives no longer but to Jesus Christ, Our Lord, who holds to Him the place of father, mother, brothers, sisters, and all things." (1)

As is seen, it is not the love of parents that religious profession suppresses; it strives, on the contrary, to render it more true, pure and real, by cutting off carnal affection which too often lessens it; and since the religious owes the plenitude of his affections to Jesus Christ, to whom he has consecrated himself entirely, it wishes that he should despoil himself of that pretended love of parents, which would be only the love of the world and of self, going back into the midst of the world, and entangling itself in the affairs and interests of the earth.

In the religious the love of parents is no longer produced by certain acts unsuitable to the perfect service he owes to God; but this

(1) Sum. of the Constitutions, 8.

love always occupies the place required by well-regulated charity, namely, the first place after God ; it is more solid and more generous than that which satisfies the world ; and it is above all more profitable to parents, because it looks first to their essential welfare, which is that of their souls. (1)

(1) We add nothing to what " The Catechism of the Vows" briefly indicates on the obligations of novices. Superiors will find the explanation of them in the "Treatise on the Religious State," by Father Gautrelet, part 1st, chapters II and III.

PART SECOND

ON THE THREE VOWS OF RELIGION IN PARTICULAR.

The second part of "The Catechism of the Vows" seems to us to call for much less development here than the first; for on one side it contains not so much the principles as their applications, which are already in the text; and, on the other side, the details which might be desired are abundantly furnished by books placed in the hands of all, as "Christian Perfection," by Rodriguez, "The Religious," by Father St. Jure, etc.

CHAPTER I.

RELIGIOUS POVERTY.

ARTICLE 1.

TWO PRINCIPLES ON EVANGELICAL POVERTY.

SECTION I.--*Evangelical Poverty attacks Cupidity, the first enemy of Salvation and Perfection.*

"Blessed are the poor in spirit: for theirs is the Kingdom of Heaven." (1) Such is, as every Christian should know, the first beatitude proclaimed by Jesus Christ, the beatitude of voluntary poverty.

This blessed poverty, to which the Gospel promises the Kingdom of Heaven, consists gen-

(1) Matt. v, 3.

erally and in its essence in the care taken to
keep the heart detached from the temporal
goods of this world; and even the wealthy who
possess these goods must have this detachment
in a first degree, in order to be able to merit
life eternal.

In a superior degree and with more merit, is
it the portion of those who accept and support
in a Christian manner the real privation of the
goods of fortune, when such is the will of God
and the disposition of His Providence.

But its supreme degree and merit shine forth
in the generous hearts who voluntarily renounce both the wealth that they possess and
that which they might acquire, in order to
raise all their desires towards the riches of
eternity. To these does Jesus Christ declare
that the Kingdom of Heaven already belongs
to them, that they have paid for it in advance
and that they have become its actual proprie-
tors by the voluntary sacrifice which they have
made.

And why is poverty in spirit the first of the
means that man must employ as well to gain
Heaven as to acquire perfection? We have
already said it, (1) and it is good to repeat it
again: because it is the remedy to that one of
our spiritual evils which is the root of all the
others, according to these words of the Apostle: "The root of all evil is cupidity." (2)

---

(1) Part 1st, ch. 2, art. 4, sec. 1st.

(2) For the desire of money is the root of all evil. I Tim.
vi, 10.

This is why the Saviour of men not content
with opening his preaching by this, also begins
His life by giving in His person this first lesson from the stable and the crib. And when
He wishes to teach the secret and the road to
perfection, He gives notice that it is still thence
that the start must be made: "If thou wilt be
perfect, go sell what thou hast, and give to the
poor and thou shalt have a treasure in Heaven."
(1) The first to receive this great lesson and
to will to practice it in its whole extent, were
the Apostles. They likewise presented it to
the fervor of the primitive Church, and have
thus given to religious communities the form
of perfect poverty. (2)

Cupidity is then the first enemy to be at-
tacked, that the soul may become capable of
rising towards God and of attaching itself to
Him: for the obstacle that this enemy opposes
to charity is of a nature to give means and
strength against it to all the other enemies,
riches being as the food and instrument of all
our passions. Hence the anathema pronounced
against the rich; (3) hence the names given to
riches—they are sources of deception, briars
and thorns that choke the good seed; (4) glue.
by which souls are caught and fastened; pitch,
the very touch of which soils the hands.

(1) Matt. xix, 21.
(2) See Rodriguez, Part III, 3d Treatise, ch. 4.
(3) Woe to you that are rich. Luke, vi, 24.
(4) Matt. v, 13–22.

SECTION II.—*Poverty is the Wall of Religion.*

This is the second principle upon which it is necessary to insist, and may Heaven grant that religious be thoroughly convinced of it and remain always penetrated with its importance.

Poverty is justly called *the wall of religion.*

The wall, that is *the foundation;* is again that *the wall of construction* of the whole edifice; again finally, *the wall of defence* and *the rampart.* The wall *of religion,* that is, of *that state of perfection* wherein one must be given up wholly to God and to His service: which must be understood of the entire *religious body,* of every *religious house,* and of every *religious* individually.

I.—Poverty is *the wall of foundation* upon which rests the two other essential virtues of the religious state—chastity and obedience. And in fact these have a need of it that is morally necessary; for, without poverty, it is extremely difficult to be and to remain perfectly chaste, humble and obedient, as is proved by the greater number of the wealthy of the world. With greater reason is poverty the foundation upon which *charity* is to rise, as we have said when speaking of cupidity, its enemy.

II.—Poverty is again the *wall of construction* of the whole edifice which chastity and obedience are afterwards to furnish and to embellish; of that spiritual edifice called a religious order or a religious house, or the religious life in the individual.

In fact, see the radical difference between what takes place here and in the world. There, if a business firm is to be founded, the members begin by considering how much money they can contribute to the capital of the company. Likewise, when the question of getting settled in life and of making a home is under study, the resources of the two parties to the marriage are first examined. Finally, to build a material edifice, money is indispensable: "Which of you having a mind to build a tower," says Our Lord, "doth not first sit down and reckon the charges necessary, whether he have wherewithal to finish it?" (1)

But, on the contrary, if a religious society or house is to be founded, the capital and funds essential to it are holy poverty, without which God and the Church would not recognize it. Does any one wish to get *settled* in religion, he must at the start despoil himself of his goods; and to raise the edifice of the spiritual life within himself, he must again and ever remain poor. "So likewise," does Our Lord add at the same place, "every one of you that doth not renounce all that he possesseth, cannot be my disciple" in the religious state. (2)

Nevertheless, some one will ask, are not temporal resources necessary also to religious societies, must not every one in religion have the necessaries of life? Yes, doubtless, what is at least necessary to the life of the body is needed; and for that very reason religious are

(1) Luke, xiv, 28.   (2) Luke, xiv, 33.

also told: Be really voluntarily poor, keep holy poverty faithfully, and God will feed you: His word is given for this: "Seek ye first," has He said, "the Kingdom of God and its justice and all the rest shall be added unto you:" (1) otherwise the divine promise is not made to you. This is why, when evangelical poverty failed in religious houses, they collapsed, God and man uniting to destroy them; God using the injustice of man for the accomplishment of His just decrees. If material edifices continued to stand here and there, they were no longer religious houses: they no longer sheltered true religious; instead of those real vocations, so numerous in times of fervor, there were seen to enter there only worldly minds and hearts, who gathered together to prey on the goods of religious and who completed the preparation of its entire ruin.

III.—Holy poverty is *the wall of defence* of religion: "Solid rampart and refuge," says St. Ignatius, "which God inspired religious orders to establish against the enemy of human nature and against the other adversaries of religious perfection; bulwark under whose shelter they maintain themselves in their state, preserve the vigor of discipline, and resist a multitude of aggressions: this makes it easy to understand why the devil makes so many efforts, and does his utmost by so many means to overthrow this wall of defence." (2)

(1) Matt. vi, 33.   (2) Constitutionum, Parte X, ₰ 5.

It is a rampart *against the world*, of which "the errors, loves and terrors," as says St. Augustine, no longer reach the voluntarily poor, because in fact, by despoiling himself of the goods of this world, he has freed himself from its seductions, its enticements, its distractions, its cares and all its embarrassments.

It is a rampart *against the devil:* for, says St. Gregory, "Satan vainly engages in contest with the voluntarily poor; he struggles against athletes disembarrassed from their garments" (1) and upon whom he can catch no hold.

It is a rampart *against the flesh itself*, notwithstanding the advantage possessed by this enemy of remaining within us. For where does the triple concupiscence find its food? In riches, since money helps to obtain everything in this world—pleasures, honors, welfare of life. And as we have said, cupidity is banished from hearts along with wealth, by religious poverty, it is impossible not only for every religious individually, but also for the commuity itself to have even the design to amass and to hoard, if poverty remain intact, for the poor are always at hand, according to the will of God, to receive whatever is superfluous. Thus religious poverty turns away the pleasures and enjoyments of life in food, clothing, furniture, etc.; there remains only what is necessary and proper, regulated and sanctified by obedience, resting on a life of penance and sacrifice wherein holy poverty ever holds sensuality in

(1) Homil. 31, in Evangel.

check. So, also, the pride of life is very ill at ease with poverty, for the latter does not procure the homages of the world nor what flatters human vanity: besides, poverty naturally helps the heart to maintain itself in interior humility and modesty.

IV.—It is then true that poverty is a rampart behind which every religious and the entire religious body are sheltered from all their enemies. Therefore have religious orders traversed centuries without suffering any harm, so long as that wall remained solid and intact, whilst, on the contrary, in all of them that have degenerated, it has always been by breaches made in that rampart that evils have been introduced. And this is why all holy founders have raised it around their edifices, why all their worthy successors and all true religious have left nothing undone to maintain it and defend it, why all holy reformers have begun by repairing the breaches in it. But this is also the reason why "the enemy of mankind, on his side," as St. Ignatius says again, (1) "never fails to attack this bulwark and refuge in an effort to weaken it; changing what the first founders wisely regulated, and introducing innovations not at all according to their spirit." These words, applied to the past, recall, alas! the causes of a long and deplorable history. Religious houses and entire orders wherein numerous Saints had been formed, were thrown by the neglect of holy poverty into a relaxa-

(1) Constitut., Part VI, c.

tion that in some of them reached even deprivation. These worn-out bodies finally fell into corruption, when violence came to make them disappear and to cast their pernicious riches as spoils to the wicked.

Let us sum up: poverty is *the wall* of religion for the organization and the members: the support and defence of the religious spirit, of every religious vocation, of every religious virtue and every religious house. With holy poverty, religious shall always find it easy to be humble, chaste, obedient, mortified, meek men, united by fraternal charity, attached to their vocation; just as religious communities solidly established upon that foundation shall ever offer a spectacle of regularity and edification. On the contrary, without holy poverty everything is in peril and the wounds inflicted upon it inevitably bring after them relaxation, decay and ruin.

St. Ignatius draws the following conclusion from this whole consideration on poverty. "We must then love it with an affection founded on esteem and preserve it in all its purity." (1) Esteem alone does not suffice, nor affection alone: it must be a love founded on esteem, *diligenda est:* for we take little care to preserve what we do not love, and are apt not to love with a sufficiently steadfast affection what the mind does not appreciate at its proper value. But, moreover, this love being

_____

(1) Paupertas ut murus religionis diligenda est et in sua puritate conservanda. Constitut., Part VI, c. 2.

thus well rooted in the depths of the souls, it will show itself by deeds: on the one hand every religious will avoid for himself every infraction, and, on the other, he will oppose with all his might anything that would lessen the first purity of it in his institute: for, finally, most witless, very blameworthy and a great enemy of his community and of his own self would that religious be who would himself demolish or allow others to pull down the wall of foundation of construction and of defence.

ARTICLE II.

THE VOW OF POVERTY.

The vow of poverty is, as we have seen, (1) the first of the three exacted by the state of perfection; and as we have also seen (2) religious make it with the purpose of attacking cupidity more victoriously, that first enemy of charity in the heart of man.

SECTION I.—*This Vow considered in the religious who makes it.*

§ 1.—*The nature and the matter of the Vow of Poverty.*

This vow may have two degrees: one which is more complete and more perfect consists in forbidding not only every act, but also every right of ownership, so that the religious can no longer possess anything as his own, nor acquire

(1) Part 1st, ch. II, art. IV.   (2) Part II, ch. I, art. I.

anything for himself, by donation, testamentary legacy, or even legitimate inheritance. He may, however, even with this vow, with the consent of his superior, accept a legacy or a donation, not for himself, but for his community. In some congregations, this same vow admits also this reserve, that the religious may acquire personally in the three ways above-mentioned, but with the obligation of despoiling himself as soon as possible of the goods coming to him, to assign them to some pious destination.

The other degree of the vow of poverty, less high and less complete, leaves to the religious the bare ownership of his goods, and deprives him only of the right of disposing of them without the authorization of his superiors, and it is by thus interdicting all act of ownership, that it does away with unregulated attachment to material things, prevents the dangers of the use of them and exercises religious in detachment from them by means of dependence in the disposal of them.

In spite of what is practiced in certain congregations which allow to their members the free use of their patrimony, it should be known that the Holy See, when in approving an institute, exacts that every act of ownership be interdicted therein by the vow, without making an exception of personal goods; and besides, here is the declaration made by it recently in order clearly to point out the practice of the vow of poverty, even in congregations wherein

only temporary vows are made : "In these institutes, the vow of poverty does not take from
the professed the power of keeping the bare
ownership of her temporal goods ; but it does
take away from her all right of administering
these goods and of disposing of the fruit or revenues which they produce, so long as she remains in the community. This is why, before
making profession, a Sister must cede, even by
a private act, the administration, use and usu-
fruct of the said goods to whomsoever she
pleases and even to her own institute if she so
prefers. But the said cession shall be null and
void in case the Sister leaves the congregation.
She may even affix the clause that the above
cession shall be always and at any time revoca-
ble, even were she to remain in the institute :
however, so long as her vows last, she is interdicted to make use of this faculty so reserved
to herself, without the permission of the Holy
See.

"The same rule is to be observed in regard
to the goods coming to her as inheritance after
profession.

"As to the domain of her goods, she shall
have the power of disposing of them either by
will, or to perform with the permission of her
superiors, however, all the acts of ownership
prescribed by law."

The rule above given, as to an inheritance,
applies equally to a testamentary legacy or to
a donation made by a person still living. It
is to be remarked, moreover, that to accept a

legacy or a donation, the vow obliges the religious to have the superior's permission; and this same permission is required in order that he may dispose in favor of some one else, of goods possessed by him as his own.

§ II.—*The violation of the Vow of Poverty.*

The "Catechism of the Vows" states the cases wherein this vow is violated, and in what manner permission is required to dispose of temporal things. Moral theologians discuss other cases upon which we think we need not enter. At the most we shall add here some points of more ordinary application.

1st. The manuscripts of a religious do not fall under the vow of poverty, unless he wishes to draw from them some temporal profit, as selling them, having them printed, etc. Nevertheless, they always remain under the dependence of the superior, through obedience, as the general welfare or the good of the individual may require.

2d. To eat or to drink at the homes of outsiders, without permission, is not only a fault against discipline, but also a real, though generally slight, violation of the vow of poverty, which forbids the receiving of anything upon one's own authority.

3d. Likewise, the vow does not allow the religious to give away without permission what the community furnishes him for his own use or needs, as an article of clothing, a portion of his repast, etc.; unless a legitimate custom has granted a general authorization for this. ·

4th. A religious who, without permission, should refuse to accept the payment due to his work, would sin against his vow of poverty, and even against justice towards the community, since the latter has already the right to this, in virtue of the principle that all that is acquired by the religious is required by the monastery.

5th. Regarding a deposit accepted out of kindness by a religious to take care of it, this is to be remarked—that the vow of poverty is not violated if it be understood that he does not contract the proper obligation of a trustee or treasurer, which is to answer for the object in case of loss. However, even in this case, it is most wisely forbidden by the rule to accept any deposit without permission.

SECTION II.—*Influence of the Vow of Poverty on the general poverty of the Institute.*

Two kinds of poverty pertaining to the vow made are found in the religious state: one *personal* to the religious taken individually; it is the only one spoken of in "The Catechism of the Vows;" the other *common* to the whole body and regarding all the religious of the institute taken collectively, concerning which it is proper to say some words here.

I.—The poverty common to the religious body is not the same in all institutes; the rule of every order adapts it to its end in the measure necessary to attain this end. The strictest is that which interdicts to the community itself the power of possessing real estate. By this is meant all goods of a nature to produce fruits or revenues capable of assuring the subsistence and maintenance of the religious. Such was formerly the poverty common to all the orders called *mendicants*, because the religious must derive their means of subsistence only from the alms of the faithful, without there being any possibility of these alms being converted into permanent possessions supporting the community. However, this poverty does not exclude the possession of the religious house with its church and its garden, except in the order of Friars-Minor, and that of the Capuchins, in which even these three things do not belong to the community but remain subject in title to the donor or the Church.

Such·poverty no doubt adds much to the perfection of personal poverty. For by prohibiting to the community the possession of real estates and of revenues drawn therefrom, it flows back on the members, who in consequence of it no longer have any means of subsistence assured in advance: which becomes also for each religious a most meritorious exercise of abandonment to providence and of faith in the promise of the Divine Master. This promise besides shall never fail, so long as they themselves shall fulfil the condition made by Him: "Seek first the Kingdom of God and His justice, and all these things shall be added unto you." (1)

II.—For wise motives, the Council of Trent (2) has authorized all the mendicant orders, except the Friars-Minor and the Capuchins (whose father, St. Francis, so loved holy poverty) henceforth to possess real estate in common: so that several institutes formerly mendicants, are in fact so no longer, although this name and its privileges are preserved to them by the Church on account of their primitive rule. Only the Discalced Carmelites and the Society of Jesus for its professed houses, have renounced the right to profit by this concession of the Council.

III.—In regard to *the perfection of the common poverty*, St. Thomas makes a distinction between the monastic institutes, the mendicant orders, and those which must exercise works of corporal mercy. For he says, the most perfect poverty is not always the strictest, but that which is most in proportion with the end of the institute. Thus it is proper, in monastic orders to have in common certain and sufficient means of existence ; otherwise they would have to be sought for out of the monastery to the detriment of contemplative life which is the end of these orders. St. Ignatius thought the same of his children who are at their studies in the seminaries and colleges, and the Society of Jesus belongs to mendicant orders only by its professed houses.

(1) Matt. ch. vi.   (2) Concil. Trid., Sess. XXV, c. 3.

As to institutes having as an end the exercise of corporal charity, the perfection of their poverty could not consist in the exclusion of common resources, since they are necessary for the service of the neighbor and the works of their vocation.

IV.—A remark *still* to be made on common poverty, is that which subjects the religious to a more entire dependence on superiors will become really more meritorious through obedience, than a more austere and painful poverty in which less dependence is found; and it will also serve more efficaciously to the perfection of detachment, in which above all consists the merit and the perfection of poverty. For instance, who does not see that if in a community in which the religious live solely by alms, superiors should allow to every member the free use of the gifts he receives, the spirit of poverty will be in far greater peril there than in a house wherein, with assured means of subsistence, everything is faithfully and even in the smallest matters sub-ordinated to obedience?

Let it be remarked, finally, for the consolation of many, that there exist, principally in our days, many religious communities, in which, without having by the express terms of their constitutions the common poverty of mendicant orders, it is in fact practiced with the merit of the same abandonment to that same Goodness who cares for those who have left all to seek the Kingdom of God and His justice.

ARTICLE III.

ON THE VIRTUE OF POVERTY.

The virtue of poverty is not explicitly mentioned among the moral virtues; but it is an evangelical virtue, which by detaching man's heart from the temporal goods of this world, calls into exercise almost all the moral and theological virtues. It relates more directly to liberality and temperance; and we know in what esteem it was held even among the wise men of Paganism; let it suffice to quote these words of Cicero: "Nothing is more honorable and magnificent than contempt of riches." (1)

The obligation imposed by this virtue upon religious is sufficiently explained in "The Catechism of the Vows," and likewise how the latter can sin against the virtue, even without violating the vow of poverty. We have only a few observations to add here.

I.—Undue affection for temporal goods and objects.

Cupidity is so lively a passion that it ever needs to be watched and repressed in man's heart. Would to God that the religious, whoever he may be, would never forget this truth attested by experience; for this inclination is not destroyed because it is chained down by the vow; and when it seeks to satisfy itself it becomes extremely fruitful in subtilities and pretexts. Accordingly, it is seen, after having

(1) Nihil honestius magnificentiusque quam contemnere pecuniam.

made great sacrifices, such as the religious renunciation, clinging often later on to trifles, and for want of more considerable objects, seeking therein its gratification. And, it should be well noticed by the religious, the object of cupidity matters little to the tempter who excites it, that the enemy of souls seeks and what satisfies him is the unruly affection; and he strives to attach the heart first to little things, in order to be able to obtain little by little more serious disorders. (1)

II.—Superfluities.

It must be remarked that that which should be so called in communities, necessarily presents more or less appreciable differences according to the various ends of institutes. It therefore does not belong to individuals to decide whether or not a thing be superfluous simply by their own estimate; things touching this matter are generally defined by the rule or the declarations of superiors, and it is the duty of every religious to conform faithfully to these.

III.—Of the peculium and other similar exceptions regarding the use of temporal things.

There are two kinds of peculiums: one which is a real violation of the vow of poverty, because it contains at bottom an independent use of temporal things; the other, which is not absolutely against the vow, because it remains dependent on the superior's will. The peculium forbidden by the vow is that for which the superior gives permission whilst renounc-

(1) See Rodriguez, Part III, 3d Treatise, ch. 5.

ing his right to revoke it when he shall think
fit, or again, when his permission is invalid,
being given against the prohibition of the constitutions. Moreover, even the peculium which
does not reach the positive violation of the vow,
is fatal to religious communities, because it does
harm not only to the spirit of poverty, but also
to fraternal union and edification. It is here
that may justly be applied the reproach addressed by St. Paul to those Christians of
Corinth who forgot the rules established in
the holy assemblies of the first Christians:
"When you come therefore together . . . one
indeed is hungry and the other is drunk . . .
is it not putting them to shame that have not?
What shall I say to you? Do I praise you?
In this I praise you not?" (1)

For further details on the question of the
peculium, superiors may have recourse to
Father Gautrelet's treaties on "The Religious
State." (2)

IV.—Of the distribution of the temporal
goods of which the religious despoil themselves
either before or after profession.

Jesus Christ, Our Lord, in giving the form
of the religious state, said in His Gospel: "If
thou wilt be perfect, go, sell all that thou hast
and give to the poor." (3) Thus it is very

---

(1) Convenientibus ergo vobis in unum . . . alius qui-
dem esurit, alius autem ebrius est. Numquid . . . con-
funditis eos qui non habent? Quid dicam vobis? Laudo
vos? In hoc non laudo. I Cor. ii.

(2) Vol. I, p. 171.

(3) Vende omnia quæ habes, et da pauperibus. Matt. xix.

noteworthy that the evangelical counsel on religious poverty extends to the very use to be made of the goods of which one despoils one's self, *give them to the poor:* says Our Lord, and not *Give them to your relations or your friends.* Would a religious after having listened to the first part of the Divine Counsel, wish not to hearken also to the second? This would be to act contrary to the perfection of his state, and to deprive himself of the merit of his renunciation, by corrupting it with a mixture of human affections.

There is, besides, a very particular reason for this destination of goods proposed to the religious by Jesus Christ, a reason connected with the solidity of his very vocation. In fact, if he gives his goods to his relations, could not the day come when he would count upon them in case of unfaithfulness to his vocation? And in time of temptation, would not the devil himself have something to use to shake and overcome him. But when a person has given to the poor all that he possessed, on the one hand, he has the right to that treasure promised in exchange by Jesus Christ, since it is to Him really that the goods have been given in the person of the poor; and, on the other, after having thus, so to speak, burnt one's ships, there remains only to cast one's self without reservation, and so to say headlong, into the career of perfection. It may thus be seen that not only is the practice of this evangelical counsel more meritorious and

more perfect, but that it is also a preservative
against one's own instability, a means of perseverance and of fervor in the service of God.

If, however, relations themselves be poor, it
is evident that it would be the duty of the religious to provide for them, even before thinking of any one else; and in the appreciation
of their needs he must moreover have regard
to the legitimate claims of their condition.

When any doubt arises, in a case of this kind,
advice should be sought by permission from disinterested, enlightened and virtuous persons:
enlightened, that they may give prudent counsel; disinterested and virtuous, that they may
give it according to God and true piety.

Other just motives which the religious should
consider, may arise in this matter: for instance,
an obligation of justice, some debt of gratitude, or even occasionally the necessity of preventing discussions, scandals, etc.

By *the poor* must, doubtless, also be understood, those voluntarily poor for Jesus Christ,
and especially one's brethren in religion. Is
it not even a duty of gratitude (more should
be said) for the religious not to forget the needs
of a community which takes upon itself the
care of him for the rest of his life?

The Gospel words must equally be inter-
preted to include all *good works:* such as the
care of divine worship, the propagation of the
faith, the Christian education of children,
assistance given to the unfortunate; and it
is as just as it is natural to help in particular

the works of the religious body of which one is a member.

Within the limits traced by his profession, the religious remains *free to follow his own devotion* for the distribution of his goods, for it is to him and not to others that Jesus Christ addresses Himself: *Give them to the poor;* and no one has the right to fetter the virtuous exercise he wishes to make of this liberty in the use of the goods given him by God.

Nevertheless, superiors have to fulfil a duty here of superintendence and direction in order to prevent the religious from doing anything contrary to edification and the spirit of his state.

V.—As to what regards the practice of the virtue of poverty and its divers degrees of perfection, "The Catechism of the Vows" gives all the principles; and although this is done in few words, nothing essential seems to be omitted. If further developments are desired, they will be found in Rodriguez "Christian Perfection." (1) It will be sufficient to add two observations.

The first is, that all those who enter religion need to apply themselves carefully, from their novitiate, to thoroughly understand what religious poverty is, and to acquire its spirit and holy niceties; and to watch over their former habits which are too often in opposition to it. Once admitted to the livery of "Him who be-

(1) Part III, 3d Treatise, chs. 6, 7, and 8.

ing rich became poor for your sakes," (1) it is no longer allowable to preserve the thoughts, judgments, language or tendencies of men of the world in regard to the riches of earth; and he who is truly poor for Jesus Christ, loves to appear so and to be so in his whole person, in all his conduct and even in the least thing.

The second observation is that in the eyes of a good religious, holy poverty is not only the wall of religion, it is also *a mother to be loved with tenderness;* consequently, he is not satisfied with bearing it with resignation, but he cherishes its livery, and is happy to catch every opportunity of experiencing its privations. "Let all," says St. Ignatius to his children, "cherish poverty as a mother, and in suitable circumstances, let them be well content to feel some of its effects within the limits of a holy discretion." (2)

CHAPTER II.

RELIGIOUS CHASTITY.

If the first vow of religion is of so great a merit before God, what will it be of the second? And if evangelical, poverty makes of the religious a man no longer holding to this earth, what will be said of that still more celestial virtue by which he imitated the very life of the angels ?

(1) Propter vos egenus factus est, cum esset dives. II Cor. 8.

(2) Constitut., Part III, c. I.

But "The Catechism of the Vows" (1) has already sufficiently explained what concerns this beautiful portion of the religious holocaust. The vow and the virtue, the direct and the indirect infractions, the necessary preservatives, the means of more and more insuring the possession of this treasure, finally, the prerogatives and the advantages of religious chastity, all seems to be therein set forth with the brevity required by the delicacy of the matter, and yet with the clearness necessary to enlighten consciences.

We therefore see nothing to add now upon this second vow of religion.

If a summary be desired of all that it requires from the religious, here it is in three words: *the guard of the thoughts, the guard of the affections, the guard of the senses;* and for further development, recourse may be had to Fathers Rodriguez and Saint-Jure. (2)

Regular discipline embraces several points having some relation to religious chastity, such as *enclosure, the parlor, visits and communications through letters;* but what is to be said to religious upon these matters is found in the rules of their institute; and as to superiors, they will consult with profit Father Gautrelet's treatise on "The Religious State," in order to have all the explanations that they may desire.

(1) **Part II, ch. 2.**
(1) **"Christian Perfection," Part III, 4th Treatise.—"The Religious," Book 1st, ch. 6.**

CHAPTER III.

—

ARTICLE I.

DIVERS PRINCIPLES ON OBEDIENCE IN GENERAL. (1)

I.—It is essential to obedience to perform the work commanded, not because it is pleasing and willed on its own account, but precisely because of the commandment and because it is willed by the superior, without which it is not an act of obedience.

Whence it comes that in things agreeable to us, obedience is generally less or sometimes null; whilst it is greater and more real in difficult things or matters not to our taste. It may nevertheless happen, before God who sees and knows hearts, that even, in the former case, obedience is not less true or less meritorious, as soon as the will is ready to obey with an equal devotedness for God's sake.

II.—To act against a command without having the will to disregard it, is only a material disobedience; and, if there be a fault, it belongs formally to another kind of sin, according to the motive or end of the act, or the intention of him who sins.

III.—An inferior is bound to obey his superior only in those matters in which he is subject to him, and in those things in which the superior does not contradict a power above his own.

(1) 2a, 2æ, q. 104, a. 2.

If the command be unjust, it is not at all obligatory, since God does not communicate this authority to men to be used for what is improper. However, it is sometimes allowable to an inferior to execute an unjust command ; for instance, when the injustice falls only upon himself and when he consents to suffer it. It might happen that a person would be bound to execute this sort of unjust command, in virtue of another obligation, as in order to avoid scandal or some other harm. In case of doubt whether the command be unjust or not, the inferior has the duty of obeying, because the right to command, which is certain in the superior, must prevail over a doubtful opinion.

IV.—To obey man for God's sake may easily become more meritorious than to obey God Himself manifesting His Will directly. The reason is that by so doing several virtues are more exercised, such as faith, humility, devotion, fortitude, etc.; and this is precisely the advantage that God wished to attach to religious obedience.

V.—Religious obedience consists in this, that man, in order to be pleasing to God, voluntarily places himself under dependence to another man in all that he may order according to the rule. But as has been said in "The Catechism of the Vows," this obedience obliges *by itself*, under pain of sin, only when the superior declares that he commands in virtue of the vow. As to what falls under the simple power of ruling further possessed by a superior in the religious family, it is justly compared with that of a father in the natural family ; although it is. to be remarked that this comparison is not altogether exact, since the command of a father always obliges his children under pain of sin, so long as its matter is just and reasonable: which does not hold good for a simple prescription of a regular superior.

VI.—*Blind* obedience, recommended by the Saints to religious, as the most perfect and meritorious, consists, says Suarez (1) in the exclusion of the prudence of the flesh, but not in that of true and supernatural prudence. For obedience being so excellent a virtue, exacts no less than all the other moral virtues the direction of prudence for its acts. But what belongs peculiarly to it is that the judgment of the prudence that guides it is founded rather on an extrinsic principal, namely the superior's judgment, than on itself in things that are not evident; and it is called blind because it then puts aside its own judgment. And it excludes it in so far as it is incorrect or imperfect and not by forbidding all use of reason. Thus, for example, it should know how to examine and see whether what is commanded is against precept or rule.

- (1) Tract. de Religione.

ARTICLE II.

OBEDIENCE COMPARED WITH THE OTHER VIRTUES. (1)

I.—Since obedience is only a moral virtue, it is inferior in dignity to the three theological virtues. But it is to be noticed that among many others it possesses the privilege of containing an excellent exercise of the theological virtues themselves.

II.—Obedience, says St. Thomas, occupies the first place among the moral virtues. In fact the greatest of all virtues is that which causes the greatest of created goods to be despised, to attach one's self to God. Now, there are in this world three kinds of goods that man may sacrifice to Divine Love. Exterior goods are of the lowest order; above them are the goods of the body; and those that excel all others are the goods of the soul, of which the will is the principal, by which man makes use of all the other goods. Hence it follows that obedience, causing us to sacrifice to God the good of our will, is by that fact the greatest and most meritorious of all moral virtues.

Let us add, with the same holy doctor, that as obedience proceeds from the reverence and submission rendered to God, in this respect it belongs to religion and to its first act, which is devotion. And religion is the most noble part of justice, which is the first of the moral virtues.

(1) 2a, 2æ, q. 104, a. 3.

Finally, the pre-eminence of obedience appears in this, that in order to obey, it is necessary to omit every other act of virtue not otherwise obligatory: for man is bound to leave every optional good work, to attach himself to the good of obedience, which is for him a duty. And let him not be afraid of sustaining thereby any spiritual loss, since obedience will compensate, by a better good, for what he would have wished to do and which omits in order to practice it.

III.—A sacred oracle declares that "obedience is better than sacrifice," (1) and St. Gregory, Pope, tells us the reason: "In sacrifices it is the flesh of animals that is immolated, whilst by obedience we immolate our own will." (2) And this is equally true of the sacrifice of obedience compared with any other, such as almsgiving, mortification, and even martyrdom; since these things would lose all their value if it were not for the accomplishment by them of the will of God.

IV.—A celebrated sentence of St. Gregory will complete the eulogium of obedience: "This virtue," he tells us, "is the only one which engrafts, so to say, every other virtue in our soul, as the gardener does for his trees,—and which, after having thus engrafted them, also preserves them there safe from all harm, in order that they may grow and success-

(1) Melior est obedientia quam victima. I Kings, xv.
(2) Per victimas aliena caro, per obedientiam vero voluntas propria mactatur. Moral. 35, 10.

fully produce fruit." (1) In fact, explains
St. Thomas, the acts of the other virtues
belong to obedience, either when God commanded directly Himself or when He expresses
His will by means of a superior representing
Him. When, therefore, these acts cause the
habits of virtues to take birth and increase
within us, rightly it is said that all this is the
effect of obedience. Similarly, its peculiar
function is to maintain all the other virtues in
that *medium* outside of which they would
perish, because they would degenerate into
vice through deficiency or excess; and this
advantage is much more surely procured for
the religious in a manner altogether special
by the obedience of every day than if he were
guided only by his own prudence.

ARTICLE III.

THE VOW OF OBEDIENCE.

I.—The vow of obedience, says St. Thomas,
(2) is the principal one of the vows of religion,
and this for three reasons:

First, because it offers to God the very will of
man: which is something greater than the oblation of exterior things by the vow of poverty
and that of the body by the vow of continence.
Likewise, all the works that are done through
obedience are more agreeable to God than those

(1) Obedientia sola virtus est quæ virtutes cœteras menti
inserit, insertasque custodit. Moral. 85, 10.
(2) 2a, 2æ, q. 186, a. a 8.

that proceed from one's own will; and even fasting is no longer pleasing to Him when it has as its only principle one's own will, according to these words of the Prophet: "Behold in the day of your fast your own will is found." (1)

The second reason is that the vow of obedience contains the other two, without being contained by them. For although poverty and continence are already obligatory by vow, they are so too by obedience, under which they fall with many more things: whence comes, that in the Order of St. Benedict, obedience according to the rule is the only vow explicitly made.

The third reason is that the vow of obedience extends properly over the acts that touch the closest to the end of religion. Now, a thing is all the better the nearer it approaches to its end.

This is why the vow of obedience is more essential to the religious state than the other two. For to observe poverty and continence, even under vow, does not place one in this state which, according to St. Augustine, is preferred even to virginity consecrated by vow. In the passage of the Gospel in which Our Lord invites to perfection, it is the counsel of obedience that is contained in these last words: "And come and follow Me:" (2) for he who

(1) Ecce in jejuniis vestris invenitur voluntas vestra. Isaias, lviii.

(2) Si vis perfectus esse, vade, vende quæ habes et da pauperibus, et habebis thesaurum in cœlo, et veni, sequere me. Matt. xix.

obeys follows the will of another. Consequently the vow of obedience belongs still more to perfection than the other two, as is taught by St. Jerome in his explanation of these words of St. Peter: " Behold we have left all things, and have followed Thee." (1) Because, says the holy doctor, it is not enough to abandon the goods of earth; the Apostle adds what is perfect, when he says that he has followed Our Lord Jesus Christ. (2)

II.—" The Catechism of the Vows " (3) strives with special care to explain everything about religious obedience, both as regards the obligation of the vow and the perfect exercise of the virtue; but it is satisfied with representing things with a just precision : for the books that religious have in their hands are full of the practical developments they still require in so important a matter: thus Rodriguez especially, explains perfectly all the points only indicated by our " Catechism." (4)

ARTICLE IV.

ON THE MANIFESTATION OF CONSCIENCE TO THE SUPERIOR AND ON DIRECTION.

The same author treats, after obedience, of *manifestation of conscience*, because it is, in fact,

(2) Ecce nos reliquimus omnia et secuti sumus te. Matt. xix.

(1) Quia non sufficit tantum relinquere, jungit quod perfectum est: Et secuti sumus te.

(2) Part II, ch. 3.

(1) Part III, 5th and 6th Treatises.

a consequence of religious obedience; now, some important explanations must be given on this subject:

I.—It must first be said, that the general doctrine of ascetic writers on the manifestation of conscience of religious persons to their superiors, cannot be equally applied to all the superiors of communities. Doubtless, whoever has entered on the arduous way of perfection should not wish to walk therein alone and without direction; and it is to aid him, to enlighten him and to preserve him from illusions, that God has given him, not only rules to follow, but also superiors to consult.

Nevertheless, it is easily understood, that a great difference is to be made in this matter between superiors in priestly orders and those who are not so. The former have the knowledge and the grace of the priesthood, both of which are wanting to the latter. The former being capable of jurisdiction and, in fact, possessing it, the religious may confide to them the secrets of his conscience under the sacramental seal of confession, whilst this is impossible with the latter.

Whence it follows that *manifestation of conscience* as spoken of by the masters of the spiritual life, is due in its integrity only to superiors who are priests, and that the others can have right to it, if right there be, only in a very much more restricted measure, called simply *direction*. To support this conclusion, we give a declaration emanating from the

Sacred Congregation of Bishops and Regulars.
In the observations made formerly on the constitutions of a community of women soliciting
the approbation of the Holy Sée, the Sacred
Congregation spoke these remarkable words:
"On account of the abuses that have crept
into this matter, it is not at all customary, at
present, for the Sacred Congregation to approve
manifestation of conscience to the Superioress;
but this only is allowed—that the Sisters, if
they so wish, may disclose their defects in the
observation of the rules and their progress as
regards virtues: for, as to other points, they
must treat them with the confessor." (1) *If
they so wish*, says the Sacred Congregation,
doubtless they who desire their spiritual
progress must also wish direction from their
superioress; but finally, if it is a point of
perfection for them, it ever remains true that
it is *an optional point and not one of obligation*
that may be imposed on them by command.
Furthermore, it should be understood that we
do not speak here of those cases in which the
religious are bound, under pain of sin, to make
certain manifestations to his superiors, and in

(1) Ob abusus qui irrepserunt, in præsens Sacra Congre-
gatio minime solet approbare aperitionem conscientiæ su-
periorissæ; sed tantum permittitur ut sorores, si velint,
pandere possint defectus in regulæ observantia, et proges-
sum quoad virtutes; de aliis enim ab eis agendum est cum
confessario.—*Analecta Juris Pontificii*, 38th Part, May and
June, 1860, Since this epoch, the same answer has several
times been made to divers religious congregations of
women, by the Sacred Congregation.

which the confessor himself should impose this obligation upon him. This happens, for example, when superiors should be warned, at least by a third party, in order that they may remove or prevent the occasion of a fall or the danger of scandal, or a serious injury to the community.

II.—It must be known that superiors are strictly bound to keep secret all the confidences made to them in manifestation of conscience or direction, whichever it may be, and that it is not lawful for them to communicate them even to other superiors, higher or lower, without the consent of the religious. They may, if it is not a secret of the sacrament, use them themselves for his personal welfare and guidance, and even for the good of the community; but under the express condition of doing nothing of a nature to manifest to others what has been confided to them.

Moreover, as the religious manifests himself then to his superior as to a *father* and not as to a *judge*, the latter has no right to use this as a starting point of rigorous measures towards his inferior, although it is sometimes allowed him to reprove him kindly, and even to correct him by some remedial and paternal penance. In a word, the spirit of love and charity is the only one that should animate the inferior and the superior in these intimate relations. The one opens his heart to find help, light, consolation; and the other welcomes him with special affection and goodness, to sustain, to raise, to encourage, and to enlighten, but not to reprimand harshly or to punish him; and he should take the special pains not to esteem the less the religious who thus discloses himself only through virtue.

———

ARTICLE V.—Conclusion.

THE GREAT MODEL OF OBEDIENCE.

This chapter and this whole treatise cannot be better terminated than by recalling the Divine Model of obedience.

1st. Jesus Christ, Son of God and Our Lord, came into this world through obedience and to obey. Let us listen to what He says through the royal Prophet and the great Apostle: "In the head of the book it is written of me: that I should do thy will, O God." (1) This refers to the promise of a Repairer, made to the first man become disobedient and rebellious. "Well! yes, O my Father and *my God*, I subscribe to Thy engagement, placed on the first page of the Book, *I have willed* as Thou hast willed, and *thy law is in the midst of my heart*." It is thus that Our Saviour was to repair by His obedience the evil caused in the world by disobedience. And behold how entire and punctual was this obedience of Jesus Christ to His Father during the whole of His mortal life! He Himself has declared " one jot, or

(1) In capite libri scriptum est de me ut facerem voluntatem tuam: Deus meus volui, et legem tuam in medio cordis mei. Psalm xxxix; Heb. x.

one tittle shall not pass of the law, till all be fulfilled." (1)

2dly. Not only did the Son of God wish, by His Incarnation, to assume a nature rendering Him dependent, and allowing Him to subject His human will to the Divine Will: but He moreover practiced for the love of us, during thirty years, the same obedience as ours, subjecting Himself to men, His creatures, namely to Mary and Joseph, in whom He recognized the authority of God, His Father. "And He was subject to them:" (2) this is the whole history of His hidden life given us by the Holy Ghost.

3rdly. Finally this Divine Model became for us "obedient even unto death and the death of the Cross:" (3) so that during His Passion, He was seen to obey with incomparable meekness and humility His very enemies and executioners: "he shall be led as a sheep to the slaughter and shall be dumb as a lamb before his shearers, and he shall not open his mouth." (4)

Behold then the living and perfect rule of religious obedience—Jesus Christ, who Himself says to the candidate of perfection: "Come

(1) Iota unum aut unus apex non præteribit a lege donec omnia fiant. Matt. v.

(2) Et erat subditis Illis. Luke, ii.

(3) Factus obediens usque ad mortem, mortem autem crucis. Philip. ii.

(4) Sicut ovis ad occisionem ducetur, et quasi agnus coram tondente se obmutescet et non aperiet os suum. Isaias, liii.

and follow Me." Ah! should we not repeat here those words of St. Paul: "And whosoever shall follow this rule, peace on them," (1) even in this world and forever and ever? Amen!

(1) Et quicumque hanc regulam secuti fuerint, pax super illos. Galat. vi.

Made in the USA
Monee, IL
06 March 2021